BizzWords

BizzWords

From Ad Creep to Zero Drag, a Guide
to Today's *Emerging* Vocabulary

Gregory Bergman

adamsmedia
Avon, Massachusetts

Published by
Adams Media, an F+W Publications Company
57 Littlefield Street, Avon, MA 02322. U.S.A.
www.adamsmedia.com

ISBN 10: 1-59869-472-3
ISBN 13: 978-1-59869-472-7

Printed in Canada.

J I H G F E D C B A

Library of Congress Cataloging-in-Publication Data
is available from the publisher.

This publication is designed to provide accurate and authoritative
information with regard to the subject matter covered. It is sold with
the understanding that the publisher is not engaged in rendering legal,
accounting, or other professional advice. If legal advice or other expert
assistance is required, the services of a competent professional person
should be sought.
> —From a *Declaration of Principles* jointly adopted
> by a Committee of the American Bar Association
> and a Committee of Publishers and Associations

Many of the designations used by manufacturers and sellers to distinguish their product are claimed as trademarks. Where those designations appear in this book and Adams Media was aware of a trademark
claim, the designations have been printed with initial capital letters.

This book is available at quantity discounts for bulk purchases.
For information, please call 1-800-289-0963.

To my mother, who, as usual, got me the job.

hooter Aspirin Count Theory Bait and Switch B
hielding Blamestorming Blitzkrieg Tender Offe
ogosphere Boomerang Booth Bunny Bozo Expl
on Brick and Mortar Brightsizing Burn Rate C
tulation Category Killer Caveat Emptor Chainsa
onsultant Chastity Bond Cherry Picking Chur
er Clickstream The CNN Effect Coattail Investir
ockroach Theory Corporate Anorexia Corporat
ester Corporate Kleptocracy Cosmocrat Cur
ading CXO Cyber Monday Cyberpiracy Day Tra
g Death Care Industry Deer Market Demall Dirt
oat Dirty-White-Collar Dollarize Dorito Syndron
ot Snot Dress Correctness Drive-by VC Drop You
ants Duvet Day E-business Earnout Eat Who
ou Kill Eco-Efficiency Ego Surfing Elevator Pitc
motional Labor Entrepreneur Syndrome Eterr
y Leave Exit Strategy Fad Surfing Fallen Ang
eatherbedding Feebate Fictomercial Financi
arenting Financial Pornography Flight to Qualit
razzing Frugging Gadget Porn Garbatrage G
or Gazump Geeksta Ghost Work Godfather O
er Golden Handcuffs Google Bombing Grass Ce
g Gray Matter Gunslinger Gun Jumping Hedon
eadmill Herd Investment Hostile Takeover Hu
red-Hundred Split Hype Cycle Inconspicuous Co
umption Insider Non-Trading Intersource Jackp
ustice Jekyll and Hyde Jet Blued Jettiquette Jo
oss Recovery Job Spill Kitchen Sink Kipper Lak
Vobegon Effect Latte Factor Layoff Lust Lipstic
ffect Low-Hanging Fruit Masstige Matador M
roject Melt-Up Middlescents Mini-Tender Offe
loon the Giant Moon Rocket Mucus Trooper Mu
islacking Nagflation Nanny Bubble Nap Nook NA
AR Effect Nasdaq Nearshoring Negative Patier
utcome Negative Profit Nerdistan New Guy Ge

Contents

Acknowledgments

Thank you to everyone at Adams who worked on *BizzWords,* particularly Katrina Schroeder for leaving in most of my off-color jokes. Special thanks to Anthony W. Haddad, a great friend and a great writer without whom this book wouldn't exist.

Introduction

In business, the way you express yourself is as important as what you can do. Just ask any techie, and you'll learn that it takes more than just a knack for computers to move up in the ranks of a high-tech firm. You've got to not only walk the walk if one day you want to be the boss; you've got to talk the talk, too.

While I don't have the time to set up job-training centers to help you brush up on your business skills, I can offer you a list of some of the newest, hippest, and most important business terms used in corporate America today. By the time you're familiar with these business words and the concepts they represent, you might just fancy yourself the savviest kid on Wall Street.

From the classic to the contemporary, I've compiled hundreds of "BizzWords" that are essential to any impressive business lexicon. Whether you have an MBA from Harvard or after six years you're still working on that associate's degree from the local community college, this dictionary is all you need to sound like a business big shot . . . now if you could only figure out how to use Excel.

419 SCAM

Another Nigerian Connection

The scam began in the early 1990s, when Nigeria's economy took a dive. Nigerian university students started using this technique to scam busi-

ness visitors interested in shady deals in the Nigerian oil sector. Now anyone with an e-mail address is a potential mark.

Why 419?

Well, "419" refers to the article of the Nigerian Criminal Code (an article of Chapter 38, "Obtaining Property by False Pretences; Cheating") that deals with fraud. The American Dialect Society has traced the use of the term back to 1992.

How It Works

The 419 scam fits into a broader umbrella of advance fee fraud. The idea is that by blinding the mark with the promise of a huge amount of money ($10 million), the little bit you asked for seems small ($5,000). It's a 200,000 percent return on investment. The mark thinks that it's worth the risk. Even if the mark dropped all $5,000 on any number on a roulette table and won, he'd only have $175,000. But, while a straight bet on a roulette table will win 1 in 37 times, the 419 scam never pays off. Except, of course, for the 419 scammer.

How to Start Your Own 419 Scam

The first thing you'll need is a database of e-mail addresses. Your job probably has one. Steal it. Then:

1. Send the addresses an e-mail in strange or bro-ken English. Make sure to use all capital letters for emphasis.

2. Promise the recipient huge monetary rewards for helping you.
3. Pretend you're a government official, a bank manager, an heiress, or a military man.
4. Tell your mark that there's $20 million sitting in a government fund, a bank account, an inheritance, or a secret bunker.
5. Explain that it only takes $5,000 to bribe a corrupt official, pay a lawyer, or keep someone quiet.
6. Promise that for helping you, you'll split the cash with them.

Now you have your own 419 scam going. Good luck.

ACTION ITEMS

WHAT IT MEANS: A to-do list in the business world

Executive Identity Crisis

Boy, it's hard being an executive these days. They're responsible for all that money, all those people. They need to find power ties and drive a car that says, "Big shot coming through." Their shoes need to shine; their hair has to be greased to perfection. They need to say things that make no sense just to sound powerful and intelligent.

And, just like you, executives can feel overwhelmed by the amount of work they have to do. They face a constant barrage of looming deadlines. And sometimes they simply forget to do something important. Executives, just like you, need a to-do list.

While to-do lists are powerful reminder devices, they have a silly-sounding name. Executives know that they can't have to-do lists. Teachers and bureaucrats have to-do lists. Executives aren't like them. They're executive. They have action items. Oh yes! Action items.

DAILY ACTIONS ITEMS FOR TYPICAL CEO

1. Wake up.
2. Shower, brush teeth, comb hair—everything Mommy said to do.
3. Have a bite of sushi for breakfast. Put on today's red power tie.
4. Drive Mercedes to office. Park in personal parking spot.
5. Tell secretary to hold calls.
6. Play solitaire on the computer.
7. Have lunch with personal assistant in motel off the freeway. Tell secretary to hold calls.
8. Have board meeting. Discreetly e-mail personal assistant naughty messages on Blackberry.
9. Tell secretary to get mother on the phone and to hold all calls.
10. Go to strip club. Drink. Call secretary. Ask her to meet at motel off the freeway.

AD CREEP

Signs, Signs, Everywhere a Sign

WHAT IT MEANS: Expanding the world of advertising to nontraditional surfaces and items

No, the term *ad creep* doesn't refer to that creepy guy who works in advertising . . . you know, the one with the surgical mask and the pinwheel hat. It refers to the increasingly innovative ways that advertisers are using to capture your attention.

From covering cars to a dancing man with a sign, advertisements are everywhere you turn. Creeping into places hitherto ad-free, advertisements are, as the song goes, "blocking out the scenery, breaking my mind." But that's just part of living in today's highly competitive business world.

Most Coveted Ad Spaces

Sure, you can advertise everywhere, as the term suggests, but there are still some places that remain ad-free to the dismay of the advertising world. Here are a few of the most coveted ad spaces advertising execs are dying to get their hands on:

- Jennifer Lopez's butt
- The Statue of Liberty
- The dollar bill
- The White House (whoops, oil companies own that)
- The Vatican

Bandit Signs

Bandit signs are yet another indication that advertisers are increasingly looking for new ways to communicate their message to potential customers. However, unlike those other ad creeps out to cover the world in signs, these bandits have taken it a step further by posting ads where the law doesn't allow.

While most of these bandit signs are placed in public areas, more daring bandit signers might just break the law even further to get your attention. Now do you know why you keep finding Chinese takeout menus on your bed?

➕ **FIRST COINED**: Steve Johnson, "Creeping Commercials," *Chicago Tribune,* March 24, 1996.

AFFLUENZA

Remember Wall Street?

Way back in the 1980s (not that it seems so long ago, considering the clothes and hairdos visible around town today), business bad boy Gordon Gekko told us

{ **WHAT IT MEANS:** Hyper-materialism that causes consumers to overwork and overspend

that "greed is good." Twenty years later, this maxim seems to be more popular with the American public than ever. Unfortunately for Michael Douglas, however, his career hasn't fared as well as greed has.

Affluenza is everywhere. Take one of my closest friends, who estimates he owes somewhere around $400 million in credit card debt alone. It's true. And he's one of the luckier ones. Just look at all those Hummers on the road. Who do you think is buying them? People who can't afford them, that's who. So they finance it.

"Bad credit? No problem, just take advantage of our 9,000 percent APR, the best in the business. We look after our customers and make sure they're happy."

Thanks guys, for helping me ruin my financial future.

And with the constant pressure to buy more, who can keep up and not go broke? Only the credit card companies apparently. (Okay, so maybe the Gates family can stay afloat as well.)

Where Can You Go for Help?
If you are tired of stressing out about how to afford that new SUV, go to *www.pbs.org/kcts/affluenza* to find out when you can catch *Affluenza,* a television show hosted by Scott Simon from National Public Radio. You can also take a test to determine your level of affluenza toxicity. Here are some telltale signs that you may have affluenza.

HOW BAD DO YOU HAVE THE BUG?
- Nikes are better because they have the swoosh.
- Chase Manhattan just sent me their special-edition pyrite credit card.
- I've been employee of the month of the local electric company three times even though I don't work for them.
- Calvin Klein personally sends me thank-you cards.
- I own a BMW but rent a studio.

➕ **FIRST COINED:** Tom Shales, "Rough Cuts from Ann," *Washington Post*, October 1979.

AGE FRAUD

Ageism

Even before *ageism* entered our lexicon, both it and age fraud were commonplace. Some would say that they were older in order to buy porn, drink booze, smoke cigarettes, get into nightclubs, receive senior-citizen discounts, or act in adult movies. Others lied about being younger for pure vanity. But there is now another reason to commit age fraud: ageism from employers.

Both the old and the young are discriminated against in the workplace. One study found that 29 percent of people had been the victim of ageism. Even Pierce Brosnan cited ageism as one of the reasons he wasn't cast as James Bond in *Casino Royale*, released in 2006—and he looks pretty good for his age. Well, there's an easy answer to this: Lie like a dog. While it might not have helped Pierce, it may help you.

Just Lie

A career counselor once told me to exclude graduation dates from my resume to ensure that it wouldn't be dismissed for a big shot position just because I was under forty. The same applies to older people looking to get into hip jobs or hip companies. Best thing to do, in my opinion, is lie. Working for Google? You should be between twenty-five and forty-five, depending on the position. IBM? Between forty and 210. While you can't say you're fifteen if you're really fifty, a couple years on or off and no one's the wiser.

➕ **FIRST COINED:** "Nigeria to Reject FIFA Charge," Xinhua General Overseas News Service, April 1990.

AIR COVER

Bombs Away

WHAT IT MEANS:

When someone in upper management agrees to take the responsibility for an unpopular decision

In military usage, air cover is the use of aircraft to provide protection against attack by enemy aircraft during ground or naval operations. In business, air cover is using executives to protect employees from blame and hostility by taking the responsibility for decisions. Ultimately, however, it's likely the executive's decision. You spent six months doing the research and writing the report, but she's the one who must sign the paper to make it so.

Taking Credit Where Blame Is Due

In some circles, what you'd be blamed for and what you'd get credit for seem counterintuitive. So the CFO tells you to decide who to fire. "I'll take the blame," she tells you. Well, only the employees will criticize her for the move. The investors are clapping their greedy little hands away at the RIGHTSIZING they believe is taking place (even though it's more likely BRIGHTSIZING). The CFO gets a raise and a few more stock options, and you're cut in the next round of layoffs.

There's always the opposite. You could end up being the fall guy, a much more public and hated position to be in. These suckers take the blame for things their superiors do. Why? Maybe there's cash. Maybe you're a zealot. Either way, just stay out of jail, or you'll be praying for a presidential pardon.

Here are a few cases in which some air cover would have probably been welcome:

1. I. Lewis "Scooter" Libby took the blame for leaking CIA agent Valerie Plame's identity. Rumors have swirled that Vice President Dick Cheney was to blame.

2. The Chinese are taking the fall for industrial pollution. Not only are some saying that they are responsible for global warming, but even the cloud of smog over Los Angeles has been attributed to them. (It's really from Donald Trump's hairspray.)

3. And the most famous fall guy of them all, O. J. Simpson. The LAPD did it.

ANGEL INVESTOR

Pennies from Heaven

WHAT IT MEANS: A single person who backs a startup

Angel investors are heavenly individuals who draw from their own personal pockets to help fund your startup. Venture capitalists, on the other hand, draw from both their own pockets and those of their associates. Therein lies the major distinction.

Not surprisingly, angel investors are a more pleasant bunch than venture capitalists, who are sometimes called vulture capitalists because their terms require you to give up a lot of your company. Angels, however, usually let you keep part of it. A nice gesture, I think.

Those looking to the heavens for money should get used to someone else having a say in the future of the company. Sure, it's your baby, but the angel paid for the brat. After all, the best way to start a company, some say, is with OPM and OPT (other people's money and other people's time).

The right time to raise the first round of money varies from startup to startup. Some companies need very little cash to get off the ground, while others need a bundle. To get angel funding, you have to be able to show that your company has an EXIT STRATEGY for the investor, often in the form of a public offering or buyout.

ANKLE BITER

There, There, Little One

Just because an ankle biter is small doesn't mean it's young. You'll find companies in their late thirties and probably older in the small-cap

WHAT IT MEANS:

Companies with a market cap (number of shares times price per share) of less than $500 million

arena. Some just can't give up the dream, no matter how far-fetched it is.

Bargains

Some say small companies are bargains. Sometimes that's true, sometimes it's not. There's really no way to tell when and if a little company will go through a big growth spurt.

It's difficult for an investor to identify small companies that have a good potential to grow in the next few years. Though there are many ankle biters on every exchange, most of them are best left untouched.

The SEC wants people who trade in small companies to remember that these stocks typically trade with very low volumes. This can make finding buyers when you want to sell and finding sellers when you want to buy very difficult. Because of this, you might have to sell lower than you want or buy higher than you want to make a trade. (See the entry for SINGLE-DIGIT MIDGET.)

ARROW SHOOTER

How Good a Shot Are You?

Most people want to believe that they're an arrow shooter. They want to believe that they have true vision

WHAT IT MEANS:

A businessperson who has a visionary idea and then projects its trajectory into the future and the uniqueness of thought that is required to set a winning corporate strategy. But people believe a lot of things. The truth is that most people in the boardroom are not true arrow shooters but more like drunken dart players, aimlessly tossing out meaningless ideas. Okay, so that's a little harsh. But it was true . . . at least at my last job.

ASPIRIN COUNT THEORY

I Haven't Felt Like This Since the 1980s

WHAT IT MEANS: A market theory that states that as stock prices fall, more and more people need aspirin to get through the day

Headaches have many causes, from good old-fashioned stress to a brain tumor (though 95 percent of headaches are no cause for alarm, so don't fret). But if there's one thing that's certain to make you reach for the medicine cabinet, it's losing millions of dollars in the stock market.

On October 19, 1987, $500 billion evaporated from the Dow Jones Index, a composite of major U.S. companies often used as a barometer of overall market performance. Around the world, it was the same scenario, as one market after another bit the dust.

Upon news of the crash, individual investors scrambled to call their brokers to sell every stock they had. This caused a selling panic that greatly exacerbated the market downturn, not to mention the lives of several stockbrokers, who were gunned down by unhappy clients.

This illogical selling was compounded by automated selling programs, which automatically sold orders when shares hit a certain price. Many market historians viewed this process, called programmed trading, as the main cause of the crash.

There have been other notably devastating stock market crashes, such as the infamous crash of 1929 and the most recent market debacle in 2001, following the September 11 terrorist attacks. But the 1987 crash, now referred to as Black Monday, remains a textbook example of how irrational panic can cause a major market collapse.

Not to mention a whole lot of migraines.

BAIT AND SWITCH

Plastic Devil

Chances are, you've been a victim of the old bait-and-switch scheme at the hands of the little loan shark in

WHAT IT MEANS:
Locking in a customer with a great deal and then suddenly changing the terms

your pocket, your credit card company. Remember that card you signed up for with a low 5.9 percent APR? Now, three vacations, four Coach purses, 200 caramel macchiatos, and five pairs of Jimmy Choos later, your $10,000 balance is accruing a good-sized finance charge every month. But that little Shylock in your pocket isn't satisfied. Like a vampire, it longs to suck you dry and that bloodthirsty bastard can, too.

The most common way that credit card companies do this is to raise your interest rates once you have a large balance that you can't possibly pay in full. And so one day you ignorantly go to the mailbox, and blissfully unaware you open your credit card bill, throwing away that other junk in the envelope, including your new terms sheet which kindly informs you that you will now be paying 30 percent APR. Of course, if you don't like it, you can just cancel your card, but this will lower your FICO score. There you are, between the devil and the deep blue sea, a victim of the ol' bait and switch.

Other Examples of the Bait and Switch

You want to purchase a new "adult" video, and your local store is advertising *Hilary Muff Live on Tour* for only $3. You arrive at the store only to find that there are no copies of this DVD left, but there are plenty of copies of *Oops! We Did It Again* for $39. After driving across town full of excitement, will you return home empty-handed? Doubt it. They do too.

You tell your date that you're a CEO and drive a Porsche. After she sleeps with you, you admit that you're a freelance handyman and drive a Ford Pinto. Zing!

BID SHIELDING

Going Once, Going Twice, Sold . . .

. . . to the unscrupulous online bidders who used bid shielding to block the competition. Here's how it works.

> **WHAT IT MEANS:** Placing a low bid in an online auction while someone else enters a bid that is high enough to discourage other bidders. At the last second, the high bid is retracted and the low bid wins.

Let's say you really want to get your hands on that grilled-cheese sandwich whose surface portrays a mystical likeness of the Virgin Mary, but you're not exactly rolling in dough. Instead of playing fair, you would place a low bid, let's say for $10, and then have a friend put in an absurdly high bid of something like $28,000. The high bid would dissuade other bidders and your bid, if you made it quickly, might win out.

Say, "Grilled Cheese"

The famous grilled cheese sandwich was sold on November 23, 2004, by Diana Duyser. She had saved the sandwich for over a decade, preserving it by wrapping it with cotton wool inside a plastic container. "When I took a bite out of it, I saw a face looking up at me—it was Virgin Mary staring back at me," the woman said during an interview after selling it online.

The fact that it showed no sign of molding or crumbling over its ten-year lifespan only served to strengthen her conviction of the sandwich's divinity. The sandwich was purchased by GoldenPalace.com, an online casino known for wacky publicity stunts. How much did it go for? You guessed it: $28,000.

Now, that's really poor bid-shielding if you ask me.

➕ **FIRST COINED**: Vaughn Jones in "Online Sales in Cyberspace," *The Journal* (Newcastle, England), February 1999.

BLAMESTORMING

Blaming the Intern

> **WHAT IT MEANS:**
> A discussion about assigning blame

There's no reason why you shouldn't use every opportunity to dodge the blame yourself and put it instead on the back of your intern. What does he have to lose anyway? He makes $13 an hour to update his MySpace profile and read about Lindsay Lohan. Soon he'll be back in college using more of Daddy's cash, anyway. So the next time a project goes awry, huddle up with your colleagues and devise a plan to get yourselves off the hook and the intern back in the dorm.

➕ **FIRST COINED**: Gareth Branwyn, "Jargon Watch," *Wired*, January 1997.

BLITZKRIEG TENDER OFFER

Eins, Zwei, Drei, I Own Your Company

> **WHAT IT MEANS:**
> A generous buyout offer that is quickly accepted

Translated to English, the German word *blitzkrieg* means "lightning war." Thus, a blitzkrieg refers to a surprise offensive that's both powerful and swift, first used to describe German military tactics during World War II. The general idea behind the tactic is to defeat the enemy by quickly out maneuvering rather than outlasting them.

The tender offer's allusion to World War II is based on the speed, effectiveness, and conquering power of the German military machine. The blitzkrieg strategy used in corporate takeovers is slightly different than German warfare of the 1940s, as no tanks, planes, or artillery are used. At least, none has been reported.

Love Me Tender

A tender offer is an offer by a company or a third party to buy a substantial percentage of a company's shares. The offer is at a fixed price and often at a premium over the current market price.

BLOGOSPHERE

Check Out My New Blog, Dude!

When the term *blogosphere* (similar to the Greek word *logosphere,* mean-

WHAT IT MEANS:
The world of Internet Web logs, known as *blogs*

ing "the world of discourse") was coined in September 1999 by blogger Brad L. Graham of Bradland.com, the world of blogs was miniscule compared to today.

Now everyone and their sister is blogging. From the boardroom to the classroom, "Did you read my blog?" is one of the most popular questions in America. And it's getting a little annoying. Though it's undoubtedly a good thing that people are writing, the bad side is that the immediacy of the Internet makes bloggers believe that they're writing something actually worth reading—which is rarely the case.

If you don't believe me, check out MySpace (*www.myspace. com*), where nine- and ten-year-olds are already writing blogs on subjects that range from what kind of bubble gum they like best to the war in Iraq. But maybe I'm just getting old and fussy. (By the way, I really like watermelon BubbleYum and, according to the last blog I read, the war isn't going well.)

The Devil's Dictionary 2.0 (*www.opendevil.org*) describes the blogosphere as follows:

A poisonous environment of methane, self-satisfaction and other hot gasses. The only creatures that can survive in the blogosphere are low-order molds, able to feed off the waste of others.

BOOMERANG

I Quit, Sir . . . Okay?

WHAT IT MEANS:
An employee who quits to take another job and then later returns to work for the company

Human beings conjure all sorts of fantasies in order to escape reality and enter into an alternate world. Some of the most common of these fantasies include sex fantasies and fantasies about money. But even these cannot possibly compare in intensity to the one fantasy that every employee has had at one time or another—the fantasy of telling your evil boss to shove it!

While this may be what you are thinking right now, make sure that if you do decide to quit, you do it politely. You never know when you might have to go back and beg for mercy.

So don't burn any bridges; you may have to cross the same one over and over again.

BOOTH BUNNY

Rascally Rabbit

WHAT IT MEANS:
A model hired to work in a company's booth during a trade show

It isn't your imagination. Trade shows are not what they used to be. You used to spend your time shoving down another free bagel while chit-chatting with other suits about college basketball. But now companies featured at trade shows are doing everything they can to attract your attention, including bribing you with scantily clad, big-busted bunnies.

How to Approach a Booth Bunny

So you want to take the model out on the town, do you? Well, a million other big shots are trying to do the same thing. Here are a few great lines to set you apart from the competition. Remember to be subtle and use business metaphors that she'll find impressive and clever:

- "You're a model, right? I mean, girls that pretty aren't in business."
- "What's your favorite position? . . . I mean, acquisition."
- "Have you ever done it reverse merger style?"
- "We're always looking for multiple partners."
- "May we go up to my room and get down to business?"
- "I would like to disclothes you."
- "I've got a really big prickfolio."

OR,

Just let her know that you've got an American Express black card and a Ferrari, and let her ask *you* out.

✚ FIRST COINED: Alex Beam, "All That Glitters . . . ," *Boston Globe,* May 1989.

BOZO EXPLOSION

Send in the Clowns

If you've ever thought that your office was turning into more of a circus every day, you're not alone.

{WHAT IT MEANS:
A rapid increase of incompetent employees at a particular company

Bozo explosions are more common than you might think. All it takes is a couple of incompetent clowns in human resources to turn your company into a sideshow overnight.

THERE'S A BOZO EXPLOSION IN YOUR COMPANY IF . . .

- The average shoe size is 40.
- Round red noses are commonplace, even when it's not hay-fever season.
- The whole sales department arrives in the same car.
- When the CEO goes on vacation, she travels by cannon.
- Your secretary, Helen, has started growing a beard.
- The kid from the mailroom rides a unicycle around the office.
- The new accountant eats fire for lunch.
- Hand buzzers never fail to get a big laugh.
- When you sniff the flowers in the lobby, they squirt you.
- Your boss has replaced her fish tank with a lion cage.
- There are new parking spaces reserved for elephants, tigers, and other exotic animals.
- Only cotton candy and caramel apples are served in the lunch room.
- The ceilings were recently raised to allow more room for employees to wear stilts.
- Juggling staplers and other office equipment is commonplace.
- New, lower urinals were installed for dwarves.

Note: No animals were injured in the making of this list.

➕ **FIRST COINED:** Though he wasn't the first person to spot a bozo explosion, Guy Kawasaki, former Apple Fellow at Apple Computer, Inc., may have been the first to publicize the phrase (in a December 1992 article for *MacUser* magazine entitled, "From the Desk of Management Changes at Apple"). Kawasaki, who is credited as one of the major contributors to the success of the Macintosh computer, warned Apple employees that they must carefully scrutinize who they are hiring in order to prevent a bozo explosion.

BRICKS-AND-MORTAR

Some People Still Buy Things in Stores

WHAT IT MEANS:
Businesses that have an actual physical location rather than a purely online presence

If it wasn't for those long Saturdays at Target with my wife, or the occasional trip to the even more crowded Wal-Mart, I might even forget that bricks-and-mortar businesses were still booming. Between Amazon.com, Netflix, and online dating services, I've got just about everything I need. According to JupiterResearch, despite double-digit growth over the past few years, U.S. online retail sales will eventually plateau at 10 percent to 15 percent of total retail sales.

BRIGHTSIZING

Being Clever isn't Everything

WHAT IT MEANS:
Downsizing by laying off the brightest workers

If you've ever been laid off and thought, "How could they fire smart, wonderful me and keep the idiot to my left?" you've just been the victim of brightsizing, a not-so-clever kind of downsizing.

One of the ways this happens is when a company lays off workers who have been there for the shortest length of time. The decision is made with the good intention of keeping employees with seniority and dumping the new blood. The only problem is that, though hard for some to swallow, these new employees, who are often younger, are typically the best trained and educated. Sorry old-timer, it's the truth.

SIGNS THAT YOUR COMPANY HAS BRIGHTSIZED

- The highest level of education among employees is now the tenth grade.
- In the lounge, magazines like *The New Yorker* and *The Economist* have been replaced with coloring books.
- In the design department, the Mac has been replaced by the Etch A Sketch.

BURN RATE

Burn, Baby, Burn

WHAT IT MEANS:
The rate at which a company spends cash (that is, negative cash flow)

Every emerging company needs to burn a lot of cash on the long and arduous road to profitability. Between startup costs, R&D expenses, and paying the staff, building a business is an expensive venture that may or may not pay off. Either way, you've got to burn some green.

The burn rate is usually calculated on a monthly basis. For example, if a company has a burn rate of $300,000, it means the company spends $300,000 in cash per month. Though a low burn rate (or no burn rate) is desirable, investors sometimes view a high burn rate in a developing company as an indicator that the company is meeting its milestones and building a customer base. Some market commentators have blamed the dot-com bust on the practice of keeping the burn rate up in order to project rapid growth (rapid growth often initially costs money, after all).

Yet most investors know that it's not just the burn rate but the way the cash is burned that matters. If the burn is going to frivolous management expenses, it's bad; if it's helping the company build its business, it's good. Then again, if the company doesn't have its financing worked out, it won't matter where the money is going because it's off to bankruptcy court either way.

CAPITULATION

Forget the Alamo

In the stock market, capitulation is

a giant sell-off in which investors sell, despite low current market prices, expecting the price to fall even further. Capitulation is marked by extremely high volume and sharp declines.

After capitulation selling, it is thought that there are great bargains to be had. The belief is that everyone who wants to get out of a stock, for any reason, has already sold. Theoretically, then, the price should begin to reverse. In other words, once you hit the bottom, there is nowhere to go but up.

CATEGORY KILLER

Say Goodbye to Mom-and-Pops

Category killers are businesses with a natural monopoly in their respective industry. Competitors

can't keep up with these giants because they just can't beat the prices these killers can offer. The best example of a category killer is the retail behemoth Wal-Mart, which stands as the world's largest retailer and second-largest corporation, employing around 1.8 million people around the world. Total sales for the fiscal year in 2006 reached $316 billion.

Since its auspicious beginnings in Rogers, Arkansas, in 1962, Wal-Mart—then known as Wal-Mart Discount City—has always stayed true to its mission to beat out competitors by offering the best prices. Founder Sam Walton understood that to become the world's largest retailer, he had to give customers what they want—a bargain. It worked. Within five years, the company had expanded to twenty-four stores across Arkansas and reached $12.6 million in sales.

And that was just the beginning. Fast forward to the late 1990s, and the growth became even more staggering. Between 1996 and 1999, sales increased by around 80 percent while the company's share price rose around 500 percent. Yes, 500 percent. Now, don't you wish you'd bought that stock!

CAVEAT EMPTOR

Sold As Is

> **WHAT IT MEANS:** Let the buyer beware

Don't like the fact that your new sweater is already unraveling? Too bad, those are just the breaks. And, what about that new car you bought that broke down right after you left the lot? Well, better luck next time, kid. After all, it could be even worse—think poor Tom Hanks and Shelly Long in *The Money Pit,* a 1986 film in which an unlucky couple buy their fixer-upper dream house, only to watch the renovations kill it and their marriage.

Latin for "let the buyer beware," *caveat emptor* means that no matter how bad the product you buy turns out to be, you're responsible. It's your fault. You should have inspected your purchase more carefully. No warranty? Then just shut up and deal with it.

Today, however, the law requires that goods must be of "merchantable quality." But this warranty can be difficult to enforce, and it may not apply to all products. So, once again, buyer beware.

ARE YOU A GOOD BUYER?

- Do you read *Consumer Reports* or take your buddy Polly's word for it? (Did I mention Polly is a parrot?)
- Did you test drive your car, or did you just "get a good feeling" about the used car salesperson you bought it from?
- Did you pick your heart surgeon based on the number of successful surgeries he's performed or because he was tall?
- Do you read warning labels on medicine, or do you think all pills are good for you?
- When buying your last house, instead of checking for mold, did you scrutinize the wallpaper?

CHAINSAW CONSULTANT

Cutting Costs (And People!)

WHAT IT MEANS: An outside consultant brought in to fire employees

In everyday life, chainsaw consultants look just like you and me. There are no outward signs of evil, no "666" carved into their scalps, no horns protruding from their heads. Nope. Like meter attendants and bill collectors, chainsaw consultants are really just normal people who happen to have a job that makes people really, really mad.

Though hired henchmen, chainsaw consultants are necessary to improve efficiency. The fact is, whether we like it or not, costs sometimes have to be cut, and employees have to be let go. For that, call the chainsaw consultants—they'll gladly cut you down.

IS THE CHAINSAW CONSULTANT AFTER YOU?

- Did you forget to put the new cover sheets on the TPS report?
- Did you spend last week planning your next vacation?
- Can your job be done by an intern, a simple computer program, or a primate?
- Do you expense escorts?

CHASTITY BOND

Protecting Your Ass(ets)

In a business world teeming with sharks, sometimes companies have to take unique measures in order to ward off an attack. One such measure is a chastity bond, designed to make the company a less attractive takeover target.

WHAT IT MEANS:
A bond that is scheduled to mature once a takeover is complete with the hope of preventing the takeover

Because a chastity bond's maturity date is activated in the event of a takeover, the company executing the takeover would be immediately forced to pay bondholders, something no company would be happy about.

CHERRY PICKING

Separating the Risky from the Ripe

Similar to the way a cherry picker chooses the ripest fruits from the tree, cherry picking in business

WHAT IT MEANS:
Picking out the most profitable customers from a large base

means selecting the customers you want, and ignoring the others. Notorious for their cherry-picking efforts are insurance companies, which stand to benefit by weeding out the risky from the reliable. However, most states have laws to prevent them from getting away with it. In the case of automobile insurance, cherry picking is prevented by laws requiring that car insurance companies cover a number of drivers with poor driving records.

So *that's* why I'm still covered!

The Bush administration has been often accused of cherry picking by focusing on information that supported an invasion of Iraq, while ignoring other information that contradicted it.

OTHER EXAMPLES OF CHERRY PICKING

- No dwarves in the NBA.
- No blue-collar workers at White House dinner parties.
- All U.S. presidents have been male, white, and protestant, save Kennedy (he was Catholic—still white and male for those of you who aren't history buffs).

CHURNOVER

Win or Lose, It's All the Same . . .

. . . to a traditional stockbroker that is, who gets a commission based upon each trade executed for his

WHAT IT MEANS:

When a stockbroker buys and sells excessively to rake in more commission dollars

or her clients. Sure, it sounds like a great business, but that really depends upon whether the market is bull or bear. When times are hard, stockbrokers can have trouble maintaining their usual turnover, which means less money than they might be used to. For these bear times, brokers may commit a little churnover by excessively buying and selling shares of clients' stock to make some extra dough off the commissions.

Now do you remember why you signed up for that Scottrade account?

YOUR BROKER IS COMMITTING CHURNOVER IF . . .

- Though the price didn't budge yesterday, she bought and sold a stock a dozen times.
- He simultaneously shorted and went and long on the same stock—about 500 times.
- She represents Churn, Over, & Bergman, LLC.

➕ **FIRST COINED:** David Henry, "High Churnover," *Forbes,* March 1986.

CLICKSTREAM

Tools, Internet Options, Clear History

┌ - - { **WHAT IT MEANS:**
The virtual path a person takes while surfing the Web

For one reason or another, we've all tried to erase where we have traveled in cyberspace. However, while you may be able to hide your clickstream from your wife or your boss, Internet service providers (ISPs) are a little more computer-savvy.

With e-commerce continuing to expand, companies are increasingly interested in understanding consumer behavior on the Internet in order to stay competitive. Who comes to our Web site? How long do they stay there? What other Web sites do they visit? Answers to these questions can help create a behavior profile of potential customers so that companies can learn more about who to target—think of criminal profiling by the FBI without all that Hannibal Lecter stuff.

ISPs track and supply your clickstream to curious companies for a price—you didn't just think they were going to give you that $9.99 DSL carte blanche, did you?

The Path of Least Resistance Makes the Clickstream Crooked

With so many links, and with advertisers knowing who you are, it's easy to go down a windy clickstream. Here's an example of my latest virtual tour. . . .

I need to figure out what *clickstream* means, so I start at Google. I then click the Wikipedia link and read the definition. I come across the term *e-commerce* as a link in the text. That seems interesting: *click*. It isn't, but then I click the *marketing* link. Interesting stuff . . . at least the first several sentences. A reference to a *Forbes* article takes me there. Boring article. Ohh! Wine club. . . .

As you can see, my research led me to the bottle again. *Quelle surprise!*

➕ **FIRST COINED:** Wayne Friedman and Jane Weaver, "Calculating Cyberspace: Tracking 'Clickstreams'," *Inside Media,* February 1995.

THE CNN EFFECT

The Fox News Effect Is Worse

{ **WHAT IT MEANS:** The harmful effect on the economy caused by people constantly watching television during a crisis or scandal

Analysts and economists are well aware of the psychological nature of the markets. Good news, bad news—the market is always responding to the times. It's to be expected, no big deal. However, in times of crises such as the days and weeks after the September 11 terrorist attacks, the CNN effect can be devastating.

If you remember clearly, President Bush urged Americans to travel, to fly, or to go out and enjoy some heavy shopping. With consumer spending driving around two-thirds of the American economy, a serious lapse in trips to Target could send our economy right down the drain. Not to mention, he said, that not shopping and enjoying ourselves would mean that the terrorists had won.

As for the "Fox News effect," well, let's just say that insanity is a potential by-product.

Most Meaningless CNN Effects
It doesn't have to be a crisis to keep people watching the boob tube instead of shopping at the mall:

- O. J. Simpson trial
- Anna Nicole Smith's death/baby's daddy incident
- Scott Peterson case
- The Olympics
- Anything related to Jacko

➕ **FIRST COINED**: Eben Shapiro, "Fear of Terrorism Is Curbing Travel," *New York Times,* 1991.

COATTAIL INVESTING

Copycat

WHAT IT MEANS:
An investment strategy that mimics famously successful investors

There's an old saying that imitation is the sincerest form of flattery. What's more, sometimes it can even make you rich. By being a copycat and following in the footsteps of the great investors, many would-be market losers have built themselves a winning portfolio. That said, this coattail investing only really works if you are mimicking a money manager or firm that has a buy-and-hold mentality. The reason for this is that the delay between when your chosen guru has made a buy and when you know about it may render the move a bad one. So, if you are going to hang on to the coattails of a short-term trader, good luck; you might lose both your grip and your shirt.

A Very, Very Nice Coat

If there was an investor to mimic, it would be Warren Buffet, the most renowned investor in history. As the world's second-richest man, Buffet's knack for picking winners is legendary. A long-term value investor, Buffet's strategy has been to buy stocks that he feels are undervalued in the market and then hold them until the market comes to its senses. Or, as he famously says, "In the short term the market is a popularity contest; in the long term it is a weighing machine." Though it sounds simple, determining the intrinsic value of a company by scrutinizing its fundamentals ain't easy. But, if you do it right, it sure can be rewarding.

Note: A $10,000 investment in Warren Buffet's company, Berkshire Hathaway, in 1965, the year he took the helm, would now be worth nearly $30 million. By contrast, the same investment in the S&P would have grown to only about $500,000.

I wish he were my dad.

COCKROACH THEORY

Nasty Little Buggers!

WHAT IT MEANS:
A market theory that states that bad news tends to be released in bunches

Savvy investors have always subscribed to the cockroach theory, suspiciously raising an eyebrow every time a company or an industry announces some bad news. "There's got to be more coming," they reckon, as if they had just seen a single cockroach scuttling from underneath the refrigerator.

Immediately following Enron's scandalous bankruptcy in late 2001, many investors expected more news of corporate crookedness would surface. They were right. In the following year, one massive corporate accounting crime after another was unveiled, from WorldCom to Waste Management, from Merrill Lynch to

Merck. Because of these so-called "creative accounting" practices—an imaginative term for financial fraud—billions of dollars were lost. Not to mention that thousands of workers went jobless, and retirement accounts were squandered.

And you thought it was a coincidence that Kenneth Lay looked like an insect.

CORPORATE ANOREXIA

An Unhealthy Diet

Sometimes in corporate America, when the going gets tough, the tough don't get going—the workers

WHAT IT MEANS:
An illogical fear of inefficiency that leads to excessive cost cutting

do. But layoffs, the most effective form of cost cutting, might make an already sick company even sicker, especially when it's done out of irrational fear rather than good common business sense.

In "Corporate Anorexia: A Dangerous Epidemic," *USA Today* writer Timothy R Carpenter (of no relation to Karen Carpenter, as far as I know) explores this corporate malady and tries to give some advice about the kind of restructuring that helps heal the company, rather than hurt it.

"Anorexia, whether it be human or corporate, is a disease, not a cure," Carpenter warns corporate big shots. "The objective of reorganization is to reprocess the work to provide more customer value and productivity, not simply to eliminate jobs. When a new hierarchy of process replaces the old one of power, the organization can be more efficient and effective in meeting the challenges of world competition."

This is easier said than done. This very international competition, says Carpenter, led Western business leaders in the 1980s to begin to cut costs dramatically, learning from the prior decade that lean production systems were needed to flourish in a new era of mass production.

"The outmoded notion of a vertical organization is seen as fatally inadequate to cope with new and more challenging markets," he writes. "But, while this might be correct, it's like converting your favorite horse to the commodity status of refined glue. Yes, it can be more efficient and profitable, but who or what will replace the horse?"

➕ **FIRST COINED:** Louise Brown, "Office Paranoia," *Toronto Star,* August 1986.

CORPORATE JESTER

A Rabbi, a Priest, and Our CEO Walk into a Bar . . .

WHAT IT MEANS:
An employee who uses humor to point out the firm's shortcomings

Corporations take themselves seriously. As well they should, considering their responsibility to their employees, their shareholders, and the public in general. But sometimes a little humor can help, particularly when it can be used as a light-hearted way of pointing out some of the company's flaws. As corporations are sensitive, a joke can be the best way to bring important issues to the table for discussion.

Being a corporate jester isn't easy. A good joke might get you a promotion, while bad jokes might get you canned. The following is an example of the absolute worst in corporate jester humor:

Knock knock.
Who's there?
Snow.
Snow who?
Snow business like show business.

CORPORATE KLEPTOCRACY

Looting from the Top

WHAT IT MEANS:

A company run by executives who steal wealth from shareholders

Every executive occasionally charges personal things to the company. It's to be expected. But when ex-Hollinger CEO Conrad Black and three of his cronies were slapped with eleven criminal fraud charges in 2005, it was for more than billing the firm for an extra martini. It was for embezzling hundreds of millions of dollars, nearly equal to the company's net income at the time. It looks like Black, almost single-handedly, took Hollinger into the red.

Over a seven-year period, reports indicate that Black grossly misused company funds to finance his extravagant lifestyle, including $1.4 million of Hollinger funds to pay for his personal butlers, maids, and chefs. Other examples of his antics include a $42,000 birthday bash for his wife, Barbara Amiel-Black, and the purchase of everything from Rolls-Royces to private jets to lavish island vacations. Black even used several million dollars of company money to buy a collection of his hero Franklin D. Roosevelt's private papers! In 2003, with help from his wife and other writers, he produced a best-selling biography of the late great president, entitled *Franklin Delano Roosevelt, Champion of Freedom.*

Black's trial is expected to begin in 2007. Supporters of Black can be found on *www.supportlordblack.com,* which appeared in 2007.

Don't worry, there's no sign-in page requiring a credit card.

COSMOCRAT

The New Global Elite

John Micklethwait and Adrian Wooldridge coined the term, signifying a portmanteau of *cosmopolitan* and *aristocrat,* in their book *Future Perfect: The Challenge and Hidden Promise of Globalization.*

WHAT IT MEANS:
A wealthy person who embraces globalization and lacks national identity

According to the authors, there are about 20 million or so of these global big shots, almost half of whom are based in the United States. Most of these international yuppies are businesspeople who embrace the idea of a global marketplace and international competiton. Though some are executives of major multinational corporations and others are startup entrepreneurs, they all have one thing in common: They tend to eschew local traditions and prefer a more integrated, even homogeneous world.

YOU KNOW YOU'RE A COSMOCRAT IF . . .

- You have more passports than James Bond.
- You speak more languages than the Pope.
- Your three favorite places to take a date are the Met in New York City, the Louvre in Paris, and Benny's brothel in Bangkok.
- You eat sushi dipped in hollandaise sauce.

CURB TRADING

Only in America

Initially, stocks unfit to trade on the New York Stock Exchange

WHAT IT MEANS:
Trading stocks after the market has closed

were sold by traders who stood outside on the curb on Wall Street. Personifying the very grit of New York City itself, these traders resisted both wind and weather, selling stocks in rain, sleet, or snow.

At least if the market crashed, it wasn't a long way down if the brokers decided to jump.

As trading activity increased, hand signals were introduced to overcome the shouting. In 1921, the operation moved inside to a building on Broad Street near Exchange Place, and the American Stock Exchange was officially open for business.

Today, curb trading refers to any trading outside exchange regulations. Under the Commodity Exchange Act and CFTC rules, curb trading is illegal. So, stay out of trouble and only trade during market hours.

CXO

Chief So-and-So

There are so many titles these days—and most of them start with

WHAT IT MEANS: A generic title for a corporate officer

"chief." Maybe that's why everywhere I go some guy refers to me as "chief" or "boss." Perhaps corporate life has spilled over into personal life to such an extent that the world has become one giant business meeting. Either way, there are so many titles that they're almost impossible to count. I've compiled this list of the ones I found.

BIG SHOT TITLES
- Chief accounting officer
- Chief acquisition officer
- Chief administrative officer
- Chief analytics officer
- Chief business development officer
- Chief communications officer
- Chief compliance officer

- Chief creative officer
- Chief credit officer
- Chief data officer
- Chief engineering officer
- Chief executive officer
- Chief financial officer
- Chief governance officer
- Chief human resources officer
- Chief information officer
- Chief information security officer
- Chief intellectual property officer
- Chief knowledge officer
- Chief legal officer
- Chief marketing officer
- Chief medical officer
- Chief networking officer
- Chief operating officer
- Chief performance officer
- Chief privacy officer
- Chief process officer
- Chief quality officer
- Chief risk officer
- Chief scientific officer
- Chief security officer
- Chief strategy officer
- Chief technical officer
- Chief visionary officer

Funny, though there are only about five distinct jobs at the executive level at most companies, there are dozens of titles. Just make sure that you're in good with the CEO or the president. (Usually, they're the same person.)

➕ **FIRST COINED:** "Unisys and Chief Executive Magazine Launch Web Initiative for CEOs," M2 Presswire, January 1997.

CYBER MONDAY

Yet Another Manic Monday

Everyone knows that the biggest shopping day of the year is the day after Thanksgiving. Hordes of shop-

pers queue outside stores and malls as if they were awaiting a U2 concert. This chaotic, yet incredibly profitable day for the retail world is titled "Black Friday." And if, as a tired, totally uninterested eleven-year-old boy, you were ever forced to go against your will with your mother at 4 A.M. to stand outside a shoe store, you'd agree that the ominous title is more than fitting.

While Black Friday represents the beginning of holiday shopping for bricks-and-mortar retailers, cyber Monday represents the beginning of online shopping's holiday stretch. Coined by the National Retail Federation's Shop.org division, the term gained popularity around 2005.

According to Scott Silverman, the executive director of the organization, 77 percent of online retailers reported a surge in sales the Monday after Thanksgiving in 2004. While it's certainly a busy day of the year for online retailers, it is actually miscredited as being the biggest. Also, despite widespread belief to the contrary, the busiest day of the year for bricks-and-mortar retailers usually falls between December 5 and December 12.

Tips for Getting the Best Deals on Black Friday

Every year, another article comes out that claims to have the shopping secrets you need for coming out a winner on Black Friday. It usually says pretty obvious things, such as go early for early-bird specials, go late for late-night specials, bring advertisements, compare prices, and do your research.

I have just one other little tidbit of advice: Don't bring your eleven-year-old son! He'll just slow you down, and yelling won't help make him move any faster!

➕ **FIRST COINED**: Michael Barbaro, "Ready, Aim, Shop," *New York Times,* November 19, 2005.

CYBERPIRACY

Apple Versus Abdul

> **WHAT IT MEANS:**
> Buying a trademarked domain name with the intention of selling it to the trademark holder

When sixteen-year-old Canadian teenager Abdul Traya was accused of "blatant cyberpiracy" by technology giant Apple, his mother should have been proud. It sure beats stealing cigarettes from the corner store, anyway.

Traya, in a moment of brilliance, bought the domain Appleimac.com. Six months later, Apple began a push to buy as many domain names related to their famously successful iMac computer and, lo and behold, they found that a schoolboy had beaten them to the punch. So, Apple did what any corporation would do: It called its cavalry to intimidate the boy into giving it up. It called its lawyers.

Not exactly Captain Hook, the so-called "cyberpirate" Traya offered to hand over the coveted domain not for a ton of money but for—get this—thirty Apple computers which he asked them to donate to his school. Instead of using this dispute as good PR for the firm, Apple chose instead to continue the fight. Eventually, the parties settled on Apple paying for Traya's legal fees (which of course far outweighed the cost of thirty iMacs) and a small undisclosed fee to Traya in exchange for the domain.

Lawyers . . . seriously.

DAY TRADING

Tradeaway

WHAT IT MEANS:

Rapidly buying and selling stocks throughout the day, trying to lock in quick profits

While day trading is usually done with stocks, other commonly day-traded financial instruments are stock options, currencies, and futures contracts.

Day traders quickly buy and sell stocks throughout the day in the hope they will continue climbing or falling in value for the seconds to minutes they own them, allowing the trader to lock in quick profits. Day trading is very risky and can result in big losses very quickly.

Brokers love day traders. The fees they rake in from the constant buying and selling is enough to keep their secret love children hidden away in Swiss boarding schools until they're old enough to blackmail daddy dearest.

While some make a killing at day trading, most probably don't (though good stats on day trading aren't available). If you want to gamble, it's probably better to go to a casino. At least the windows don't open, and defenestration never seemed like a good way to go, anyway.

⊕ FIRST COINED: Tim Metz, "Risk Arbitragers Taking Beating in Recent Market," *Wall Street Journal,* October 6, 1981.

DEATH-CARE INDUSTRY

The More the Merrier

WHAT IT MEANS:

The industry that is comprised of cemeteries, funeral homes, and suppliers of funeral-related products

Sadly, the bills won't stop piling up, even when you're dead. On the bright side, however, you don't have to pay them.

The graying population in America has the death-care industry licking its chops at the morbid monetary possibilities. Despite the rising life expectancy in the United States, eventually members of the 78-million-strong baby boom generation will inevitably meet their maker.

It remains to be seen if profits for businesses in the death-care industry will rise despite the current slowdown in actual deaths. Other than the dearth of deaths, another damper on the industry's profitability is the heavy scrutiny caused by the public scandals and financial troubles by the leading company, Service Corporation International (SCI).

Funeralgate

In the late 1990s, SCI was involved in a scandal in which remains were desecrated in a company-owned cemetery. The cemetery was "recycling" graves: removing the remains of previous burials and placing other people in them.

SCI's chairman, Robert Waltrip, was a friend of George H. W. Bush's family and had made a number of campaign contributions to the Bush family over the years.

The scandal grew when Eliza May, a director with the Texas Funeral Service Commission, was fired while investigating SCI. In a lawsuit, she alleged that she was fired because she refused to stop the investigation despite pressure from the governor at the time, George W. Bush.

May's lawyers tried to compel Bush to testify at the trial, but Texas Judge John K. Dietz threw out the subpoena that would have required Bush to give a deposition.

More dirty dealings of SCI hit the news. Two cemeteries in Florida owned by SCI were also desecrating cemeteries and recycling graves. In one instance at Menorah Gardens, a Jewish cemetery, SCI employees allegedly desecrated graves and left corpses in the woods where they were devoured by wild hogs.

The manager of Menorah Gardens, Peter Hartman, died by apparent suicide in December 2001.

It is unknown if he is buried in a recycled grave.

➕ **FIRST COINED**: Margaret Engel, "The New Rites of Death," *Washington Post,* June 1984.

DEER MARKET

Caught in the Headlights

> **WHAT IT MEANS:**
> A stagnant market, neither bull nor bear

A deer market is when investors are indecisive, unwilling to make a move to either sell or buy, and the market moves neither up nor down, just stays flat, frozen like a deer in headlights.

When you see a deer market, cover your brakes and get ready to swerve. An estimated 350,000 deer per year are involved in car accidents, but far more investors can be nailed by a deer market that suddenly turns bear. Beware.

Nature, like the stock market, isn't some Hollywood production in which everyone gets rich and lives happily ever after. It's a bear-eat-bull-eat-deer world out there. If you end up overexposed on the wrong side of the food chain, you're someone else's lunch.

Rejected Names for the Deer Market

Gerbil market . . . Richard Gere allegedly stole the mascot.
Cow market . . . Vegetarians protested this name.
Chihuahua market . . . Investors turned tail and ran from it.
Rat market . . . Lawyers sued for copyright infringement.
Cock market . . . Hens sued for discrimination.

A Grave Situation

Another time investors are very hesitant to enter or leave the market is a graveyard market. In a graveyard market, investors can't get out without accepting huge losses, and the investors who aren't in it don't want to be. The market is termed a *graveyard market* because those on the inside cannot get out, and those on the outside have no desire to get in.

Like a cemetery, a graveyard market is a sad place to be. The corpses of many astute investors and brokers are buried there, and those who have survived have run for the hills, as if the bodies of the deceased still carried the bubonic plague.

While cemeteries can be beautiful places, graveyard markets are not. They are characterized by empty factories and office buildings, high unemployment, and tremendous fear. Not even grave robbers dare enter a graveyard market.

"The graveyards are full of indispensable men."

Charles de Gaulle

"Before you embark on a journey of revenge, dig two graves."

Confucius

"Procrastination is the grave in which opportunity is buried."

Unknown

DEMALL

Let's Like, Go to the Like, Outside Mall, Like . . .

WHAT IT MEANS:
To convert an indoor mall into an open-air shopping center

Malls are an integral part of American culture. They're like baseball, apple pie, and short-sighted foreign policy. What would a Sunday be without the mall? Where would we go shopping? Where would we see movies? Where would we be able to buy a delicious hot dog on a stick from a high school kid dressed in a clown suit?

Well—and I know this may come as a shock to you—you can do all those things on the outside too (save the hot dog on a stick—though they should really consider expanding to outdoor locations).

In California and other sunny states, real estate developers are fast realizing that people like to promenade outside just as much as indoors. Who knew? To fill this need, many malls are now being converted to outdoor shopping areas.

Other Businesses Converting to Outdoors

Triage centers: Inspired by journal entries of Civil War soldiers. Amputations are common and make for interesting entertainment for passersby.

Stationery stores: Really starting to catch on in the Windy City.

Strip clubs: No more drink minimum to catch a glimpse of what's inside.

Photo development stores: They should do most business at night.

The U.S. Congress: Now everyone can really see what goes on.

➕ **FIRST COINED:** Marci McDonald, "The Pall in the Mall," *U.S. News & World Report,* October 1999.

DIRTY FLOAT

Floating Versus Fixed

WHAT IT MEANS:

A floating exchange rate in which the government occasionally intervenes

There are two kinds of currency systems or "regimes" at work in today's world. There are floating currencies, and there are fixed currencies. In a floating currency regime, the foreign exchange market determines the currency's value. In a fixed regime, governments peg the currency's value to the value of another country's currency (or several different currencies) or another measure of value, such as gold. Both fixed and floating regimes can be useful, though it is generally believed that a floating exchange rate better protects against shocks in the economy and foreign economic cycles.

Even countries that use a floating currency sometimes intervene to try and change the value of their currency. This "dirty" behavior is employed when the government becomes worried that its currency is in jeopardy of going too high or too low. Instances of this might involve a powerful hedge fund that, betting the currency will depreciate, shorts massive amounts of the nation's currency. To prevent devaluation, the country may buy back a large amount of its money. This will eat up its reserves of foreign cash and/or gold.

DIRTY-WHITE-COLLAR

Henry "The Fuhrer" Ford

WHAT IT MEANS:

A corrupt businessperson

Ask someone to name a famous crooked businessperson and they'll probably name Enron's Kenneth Lay, WorldCom's Bernard Ebbers, or maybe the Junk Bond King, Michael Milken. But, despite the bad press they deservedly get, there's one prince of American industry that may be the biggest criminal of all. His name was Henry Ford.

On the surface, Henry Ford, founder of the Ford Motor Company, seems like a pretty good guy. He astonished the world in 1914 by offering a $5-per-day wage, more than double the rate at the time, and his innovations to mass production made him renowned as one of the founders of the assembly line. But there was more to Ford than just cars, philanthropy, and his squeaky-clean image—something that dirtied his pristine white collar. Don't know? Haven't a clue? Well, how's this: He was a friggin' Nazi!

By 1920, Henry Ford went public with his anti-Semitism. That year, he began his anti-Jewish crusade in the pages of his newspaper, the *Dearborn Independent,* which featured writings from the infamous *Protocols of the Learned Elders of Zion* and other classic Jew-hating favorites.

Ford's particular taste in literature didn't go unnoticed by other prominent anti-Semites like Adolf Hitler, whose love of automobiles was rivaled only by his hatred of Jews. The Austrian lunatic kept a picture of Ford hanging on his wall, and he modeled the Volkswagen or "people's automobile" after Ford's famous Model T.

Oh Henry. . . .

✚ **FIRST COINED**: Donn Downey, "Plain Murder Is Nothing Like Agatha Christie," *The Globe and Mail,* February 1980.

DOLLARIZE

Poor George Washington?

Despite its recent woes, the U.S. dollar still reigns supreme because of its long-term stability. Many developing nations tie their currency exchange rate to the U.S. dollar. Some even use the dollar itself. These countries tend to be broke-ass countries that often get aid from the United States. By ditching their own monetary policy, these countries are effectively saying "We're too dumb or corrupt to do it ourselves."

International Econ 101

A monetary policy is the way in which a nation manages the money supply in order to, among other things, constrain inflation or deflation, maintain an exchange rate, and boost economic growth. In order to maintain a pegged exchange rate, the central bank of a country that is pegged to the dollar buys and sells its own currency on the foreign exchange market in return for the currency to which it is pegged.

As for the recent woes experienced by the U.S. dollar, some say its decline is short-term, while others believe that a fundamental shift in the foreign exchange markets has occurred and that the dollar will no longer be the currency to watch. Many countries have already pegged their currency to the powerful euro, particularly Eastern European countries and those looking to join the EU. Major factors that will affect the currency markets will be if huge and growing China stops the peg to the dollar and re-floats its currency. This "de-dollarization" may have tremendous implications.

THREE EASY WAYS YOU CAN HELP THE DOLLAR

1. Don't buy imports.
2. Don't travel.
3. Don't save any money.

Actually, screw the dollar. New list . . .

HOW TO SAVE YOUR OWN ASS IF THE DOLLAR COLLAPSES

1. Buy shares of foreign companies.
2. Buy bonds of foreign countries.

3. Buy euros and save them in a German bank account. Heil Kapitalismus!

Consider this: If you buy a bond valued in euros and the dollar drops against the euro, you make the difference in dollars when you convert back to dollars. So, even before you factor in your interest, you make money. Put that in a dollarized country or the United States, and you only make the interest. However, if the euro goes the other way and declines against the dollar, you could end up on the losing side of the exchange rate.

CURRENCIES NOT TO BET ON . . .
- Argentinean dollar
- Russian ruble
- Mexican peso
- Iraqi dinar
- Monopoly money

DORITO SYNDROME

Forest for the Trees

WHAT IT MEANS:
The feeling of dissatisfaction and mental bloatedness you get after spending an excessive amount of time performing a task that has no benefit

Too much information can be disorienting. While this has always been true, the Internet has taken the Dorito syndrome to new heights. In one session, you can see twenty-five MySpace profiles, thirteen YouTube movies, and nine blogs. By the time you're finished, you're mentally exhausted. And what did you learn during this time? Not a thing. You've completely wasted your time.

Like when you fill yourself up on Doritos, you're a little sick, you're still hungry, and you've had nearly no nutritional intake besides 8 percent of your daily recommended dose of phosphorus.

45

Defeating the Dorito Syndrome

First, you need to moderate your information intake. Your brain isn't sharp enough to take in so much, so stop it. You can't spend all day watching television while surfing the Internet and talking on the phone. You're a person, not a cyborg.

Second, you need to filter out the information more quickly and efficiently that you're not interested in. For instance, if you're looking for a date online, skip the height, weight, and color and just make sure the person is rich and divorced.

DOT SNOT

Worse Than Yuppies

In the 1980s, the word *yuppie* entered the American lexicon. Short for "young, urban profes-

> **WHAT IT MEANS:**
> A young, arrogant person who got rich by owning a dot-com company

sional," the term was usually wielded as an insult to describe an immature, greedy individual whose one and only goal was to make money to buy things. Such a descriptive term still conjures up images of stockbrokers driving Porsches, snorting cocaine, and listening to Huey Lewis's "Hip to Be Square" while petting their Vietnamese pot-bellied pigs. In any event, it was a popular term.

Unlike the 1980s yuppie who is classically depicted as a slick-talking stockbroker, the dot snot is usually a little more on the nerdy side, a mix between a huckster and a computer geek. But like it or not, some of these punks run the show, though after the dot-com bubble burst many were quickly humbled.

ARE YOU A DOT SNOT?

- Do you have over 500 domain names?
- Could you trade your watch in for a down payment on a house (even in California)?

- Do you try and look tough by referring to people as "chief" or "boss"?
- Do you drive a Bentley and always take up two parking spots?
- Do you call your forty-year-old male colleagues "pops"?

➕ **FIRST COINED**: John C. Dvorak, *PC Magazine* "Inside Track," May 2000.

DRESS CORRECTNESS

You've Come a Long Way, Baby

Women have made tremendous strides in corporate America since the women's liberation movement

{ **WHAT IT MEANS**:

The style of dress considered appropriate for ambitious businesswomen

began in the 1960s. But it's still very much a man's world, particularly at the highest levels of corporate governance. This disadvantage means that women have got to be at the top of their game to get ahead, and this means not just playing the part, but looking the part, too. This means fewer miniskirts (no matter how nice your legs are) and more power suits.

Do I Look Fat in This Power Suit?

But that doesn't mean you can't be sexy. Remember, studies have shown over and over again that more physically attractive people (both men and women) fare better in their careers. Why? Because no matter what the industry, people like to look at good-looking people. So, if you've got it flaunt it; just do it in a subtle, professional way.

ARE YOU ACTING TOO SEXY?

- You enter a board meeting in slow motion, licking your lips and tossing your hair.

- On a trip to Las Vegas, not everything you did with your colleagues stayed there.
- You totally misunderstood that "oral" presentation assignment.
- At the last Christmas party you refused to get off Santa's lap.
- On casual Friday, you wear a teddy.
- You wield a whip during employee performance reviews.
- When you have too much cleavage, you make jokes about "the twins."
- You purposely wear white on a rainy day.
- When you agree with proposals during board meetings, you purr.
- You come to work naked on the back of a tiger.

➕ **FIRST COINED:** Amanda Spake, "Dressing for Power," *Washington Post,* January 1992.

DRIVE-BY VC

Would You Like Some Advice with That?

{ **WHAT IT MEANS:**

A venture capitalist who supplies money to a new company, but nothing else

In the 1990s, there was no happier place than Sand Hill Road, home to a famously high concentration of venture capitalists (VCs). Located at the center of the technology boom in Silicon Valley, these venture firms made a ton of cash by bankrolling unknown startups, many of which went on to became household names.

In this time of plenty, some VCs developed a reputation for providing little more than just a check, and neglected their role as an active player in the company. "They drive by, throw out the money, and attend the board meetings by telephone," explains Chuck Martin in "OC's Venture Capital Dean," *Orange County Business Journal*, July 24, 2000. "That is not very good."

Indeed. This is good for neither the young companies nor the venture capitalists that back them, whose successes are one and the same. Many of these drive-by VCs learned that lesson the hard way after the dot-com boom busted, when they lost an unfathomable amount of cash in failed opportunities virtually overnight. Today, in the much smaller world of venture capital, VCs are wary of spreading themselves too thin. In this most high-risk yet potentially rewarding investment game around, venture capitalists remain extremely selective in the companies they invest in—about one in 400 they see.

➕ **FIRST COINED:** Chuck Martin, "OC's Venture Capital Dean," *Orange County Business Journal*, July 2000.

DROP YOUR PANTS

Dropping Trou

{ **WHAT IT MEANS:**
Lowering the price of a product to close a sale

If you've ever been caught with your pants around your ankles, you may or may not have been embarrassed (it depends on what Mother Nature has given you, and of course your overall attitude toward exhibitionism). But as every salesperson knows, sometimes dropping your pants and exposing yourself to the world is par for the course in order to close a tough sale.

Salespeople know that it's better to make a sale than to go home empty handed, even if the commission is a little lower than it should be. The fact is that some customers are tough negotiators and inherently suspicious of salespeople. And not everyone needs boating insurance anyway.

DUVET DAY

No More Faking a Cough

Everyone has called in with a phony cough or snivel to get out of going in to work. Some people

may have even gone so far as to say a loved one died, they've been diagnosed with a terrible illness, or that they hit a twelve-year-old with their pickup. (Okay, maybe that's just me.) Either way, we've all gone through the silly experience of lying to get out of a day of work. Thankfully, however, many forward-thinking employers recognize that sometimes employees need to take a duvet day—no matter what the reason.

How to Get out of Work . . .

Not everybody works in a place where they have duvet days. After you've used the "I don't feel well" lie, try some of these more colorful excuses to avoid the office. Trust me, they'll work:

- I woke up to find a horse's head in my bed.
- I just found out I was adopted and who my real parents were. My father's last name was Stalin, first name Joseph.
- I have some classified business in Iraq to attend to.
- I woke up to find that I had turned into an insect.
- My little boy, Ricky, has the plague.
- My dog was bitten by a mailman.
- A Cessna crashed into my apartment building.
- I have to answer some tough questions by some mean-spirited Spanish priests.

✚ **FIRST COINED:** David Sumner Smith, "How to Stay Forever Young," *Sunday Times,* June 1998.

E-BUSINESS

Everyone's Going E-Nuts

E-business, in the same vein as terms like *e-mail* and *e-commerce,* doesn't just mean buying and selling online. It also refers to servicing customers and collaborating with business partners. Businesses big and small have had to rethink their businesses in terms of the Internet and its capabilities.

IBM was one of the first companies to use the term, when, in October 1997, it launched an advertising campaign built around it.

While many e-concepts and e-businesses have caught on, others have sunk. Here are some of the clunkers.

WORST E-CONCEPTS

- **E-sex:** Nine out of ten respondents reported that this idea left them unsatisfied.
- **E-BMW:** While people enjoyed the wild array of colors and models offered, no one was able to get to work on time.
- **E-cohol:** One man said he'd rather drink Listerine.
- **E-xercise:** People complained that mouse-click calisthenics hurt their fingers and required too many reps to see results.
- **E-God:** Participants reported that the Internet was too loaded with dogma.

WORST E-BUSINESSES

- **Icecream.com:** Customers complained of a melting problem.
- **Methhouse.com:** The Feds found them three hours after the site launched.

51

- **Pumpanddump.com:** The SEC indicted the company after only one quarter.
- **DrinkRioGrande.com:** Eight out of ten Americans (four out of ten Californians) developed digestion problems.
- **Nuke2u.com:** The company's Second Amendment argument didn't hold up in court.

EARNOUT

Nice Company, Now Prove It

WHAT IT MEANS:

When a seller of a business gets future compensation if the business achieves its financial goals

If an entrepreneur is trying to sell a business for $2 million (based on projections) but a buyer is willing to pay only $1 million (based on historical performance), an earnout could help facilitate a deal. If the company performs as the entrepreneur predicts, he or she will receive more than the buyer's offer, based on a percentage of the sales or earnings.

Nearly 50 percent of small-business purchases involve earnouts, which typically last two to four years and are worth 15 to 30 percent of the purchase price. Earnouts are particularly common for high-growth companies as well as companies with unproven products. Takeovers of service businesses, where the entrepreneur's relationships with clients are important, are also likely earnouts, since the buyer doesn't want the entrepreneur to simply disappear with the check. Of course, in business, people's loyalties are directly tied to the size of their paychecks, so an earnout is the only way to keep the former owners in town. They'd rather be in Hawaii or starting a new business than working for someone else. Who wouldn't?

"Entrepreneurs and their small enterprises are responsible for almost all the economic growth in the United States."

Ronald Reagan

"I'm convinced that about half of what separates the successful entrepreneurs from the non-successful ones is pure perseverance."

Steve Jobs

"Innovation is the specific instrument of entrepreneurship . . . the act that endows resources with a new capacity to create wealth."

Peter Drucker

EAT WHAT YOU KILL

How Hungry Are You?

{WHAT IT MEANS: Paying employees based on performance}

Commission. It's one of the most frightening words in the business lexicon. Perform well, and get paid a bundle. Perform poorly, and you're out on your tuckus. But that's business, especially on Darwinian Wall Street, where only the fittest survive. Nowhere is the eat-what-you-kill philosophy harder at work. In fact, you can say that it's this very philosophy that defines it.

Should You Be a Stockbroker?

If you think that you would be right for this eat-what-you-kill world, read the following passage from *The Profit,* by Kehlog Albran. The Master's wisdom will never lead you astray.

A scholar then asked:
Could you advise me of a proper vocation, Master?

He then said:
Some men can earn their keep with the power of their minds.
Others must use their backs and hands.
This is the same in nature as it is with man.
Some animals acquire their food easily, such as rabbits, horses, and elephants.
Other animals must struggle for their food, like flamingos, moles, and ants.
So you see, the nature of the vocation must fit the individual.

But I have no abilities, desires, or talents, Master, the man sobbed.

Have you thought of becoming a stockbroker? the Master queried.

✚ **FIRST COINED**: Joseph Klock, Jr., "Collegiality Revisited," *The American Lawyer*, September 1987.

ECO-EFFICIENCY

A Greener Globe

WHAT IT MEANS:
Manufacturing goods with as little effect on the environment as possible

After even ex-oilman President George W. Bush announced in his 2007 State of the Union Address that we are "addicted to oil," the problem of American oil dependence can no longer be denied. And, as President Al Gore's (well, should have been anyway) Oscar-winning documentary

54

further illustrated, the need to become eco-efficient in order to save our planet is *An Inconvenient Truth* that we must meet head on. (Al Gore went on to win the Nobel Peace Prize, and Bush, well, we know how that turned out.)

To meet this challenge, many companies are developing products with both economics and the environment in mind. An integral part of becoming eco-efficient is reducing fossil-fuel emissions by embracing alternative energy sources, such as fuel cell, solar, and wind power. Even ethanol, which is still dirty compared to those three cleaner sources, is a major step toward a greener globe compared to filthy, crude gasoline.

While conventional wisdom says that you can either make money or save the planet, that's simply not true, as the rapidly growing alternative energy market shows. Investors who are looking to make a lot of green should be analyzing young, promising alternative energy companies. The market for them has never been riper.

✚ **FIRST COINED:** "Environment Watchdog Body in UAE Soon," *Moneyclips,* April 1992.

EGOSURFING

Google Me

We've all tried to search our names to see if something about ourselves comes up. Even my fourteen-year-

{**WHAT IT MEANS:** Searching the Internet for your name or your business name

old neighbor recently searched his name on Google, only to be surprised when he didn't come up. But what was he expecting? Did he really think that his last-minute victorious bout over a stubborn pimple would be of public interest? Or the time he ate bubble gum from a senior's shoe for $3?

Other notables of the same name, however, included a convicted pimp, a billionaire hedge-fund manager, and a world-class bowling champion.

I'll admit that even I've done it. And, though when searching "Gregory Bergman" I am the first name to come up (thanks to Barnes & Noble.com), there's only about three mentions of me from a total of over a million results, most of which include thousands of lawyers, a few rabbis, and a ton of information on Ingrid and Ingmar Bergman films.

➕ **FIRST COINED**: Gareth Branwyn, "Jargon Watch," *Wired* , January 1997.

ELEVATOR PITCH

Gone in 30 Seconds?

In the fast-paced world of business, big-shot venture capitalists and other investors don't have time

> **WHAT IT MEANS:**
> A business pitch that can be delivered in the span of an elevator ride

to hear the specifics of bad ideas. This means that enterprising businesspeople must get their elevator pitches down pat and be able to deliver their ideas in 100 to 150 words, or about half a minute.

One example of a great elevator pitch is in the film *Working Girl,* starring Melanie Griffith. In one of the most pivotal scenes of the movie, Staten Island's struggling hero Tess finally gets her chance to tell big shot Mr. Trask that it was her idea to buy the radio station all along. Literally done in an elevator, this scene is a classic elevator pitch if there ever was one.

WORST ELEVATOR PITCHES

1. Virtual house-painting service
2. Kosher ham

3. George Foreman grill phone: "Cook a hamburger and talk at the same time."

4. North Korean Air: Only one-way tickets available.

EMOTIONAL LABOR

Empathy for Hire

{ **WHAT IT MEANS:**
Jobs that require employees to express false or exaggerated emotions

While many of us are paid by the hour, some of us are paid by the tear. Still there are others who must suppress their emotions and remain stoic in trying circumstances in order to get the job done. Finally, there are those that have no emotions at all and choose their careers accordingly.

JOBS THAT REQUIRE STOICISM
- Police officer
- Doctor/nurse
- Firefighter
- Any player for the Chicago Cubs
- Beefeater

JOBS THAT REQUIRE EMOTIONAL EXPRESSION
- Actor
- Terrorist (a very emotional bunch)
- Professional divorcee (you've got to win the jury over somehow)
- Politician (all that "My fellow Americans" crap)
- Opera singer

JOBS FOR THE INTRINSICALLY EMOTIONLESS
- IRS agent
- Computer programmer
- DMV worker (though they can be nasty)

- Tollbooth operator
- Meter attendant

Coping with Emotional Labor

While all jobs are stressful, those that require emotional labor can really take their toll. Here are some ways to cope if you find yourself emotionally burnt:

- Go for a run.
- Take up boxing.
- Drink a pint of gin.
- Enjoy a gallon of gin (depending on your tolerance).
- Visit Rwanda and realize things could be worse.
- Watch a comedy.
- Take a bubble bath.
- Hire an escort.
- Call Dr. Kevorkian.

➕ **FIRST COINED:** "Notable Books of the Year," *New York Times,* December 1983.

ENTREPRENEUR SYNDROME

CEO Knows Best

We've all heard the old adage, "if you want something done right, you've got to do it yourself." But some entrepreneurs tend to take

┌ **WHAT IT MEANS:**
When entrepreneurs believe that they are the only ones who can do anything right when it comes to their business

this to heart more than others. Maybe it's because they got burned one time when they entrusted an important task to a midlevel employee, only to find that it wasn't completed to satisfaction. Or maybe they're still stinging from that time they paid their neighbor's thirteen-year-old kid $1,000 to design their Web site, only to find that what they got looked like, well, a thirteen-year-old made it. Truthfully, when it comes down to it, entre-preneur syndrome is a hop, skip, and a jump to high blood pressure, loss of social life, and even divorce. It's probably better to be a KIPPER instead.

YOU MIGHT HAVE ENTREPRENEUR SYNDROME IF . . .

- You have three lawyers because you don't trust any of them. But even after paying thousands of dollars in legal fees to get an employment contract, you decide you'd be better off downloading a free legal form from the Internet and editing it yourself.
- You owe $7,000 in medical bills because you tried to fix that electrical short yourself, despite having no training as an electrician.
- You pick up the wrong kids from school because it's been so long since you've seen them.
- You find yourself staying late to mop the floors after the cleaning service left because they just didn't do it right.

ETERNITY LEAVE

Death Be Not Proud . . .

. . . nor does it have to be finan-cially devastating. Sure, there are the funeral costs (you don't want your loved one to be buried like Mozart) and all the other unavoidable expenses, but paying a lot for a proper death is one thing—losing out on even more cash while taking care of someone who is dying is something else.

WHAT IT MEANS:
Paid leave for an employee who needs to provide full-time care for a dying spouse or family member

Some employees are given a terrible dilemma. Help take care of a dying spouse or family member and go broke doing it, or try to work while the person slowly slips away. It's an awful choice, which, thanks to increasing eternity leave policies, many distressed employees now don't have to face.

Eternity leave, a takeoff on "maternity leave," is far from the norm. This is bad news, especially when you consider the combination of our aging population and our growing health-care crisis. Unfortunately, it will be the sons and daughters of the baby boomers who will be burdened with taking care of their aging parents. And, without eternity leave, there is little chance that most of these hard-working professionals can bear the cost.

✚ **FIRST COINED**: Judy Creighton, "Woman Campaigns for 'Eternity Leave' for Caregivers," Canadian Press Newswire, March 9, 1999.

EXIT STRATEGY

Sayonara Shareholders

{ **WHAT IT MEANS**: A means of escaping your current situation

In business, as in war (we've found this out the hard way) an exit strategy is crucial. It shows that you're in control of your business, that you have a plan, and that you're organized.

The most common exit strategy is to pass on your ownership stake in the business to someone else. But whether you plan on selling it whole, breaking it off into pieces, or giving it away to your nephew, it's important to know what your business is worth. Make sure to do a thorough valuation.

The most bizarre exit strategy? The feeling of waking up after a one-night stand and discovering that you are beside someone who is so physically repulsive that you would gladly gnaw off any of your limbs that the person is sleeping on just to slip away without being discovered. Desperate times lead to desperate measures. Trappers used to find a coyote foot in their trap. Apparently, the coyote would be so desperate to escape it chewed off its own limb. That's why they call it "coyote ugly."

FAD SURFING

All the Rage

{WHAT IT MEANS:

Adopting one fashionable management style after another

In the corporate world, fads come and go just as often as they do in junior high. While you may not find hip-hugger jeans, excessive face piercings, or T-shirts that say things like "Baby Girl," "I like sex," or "Juicy" in the boardroom, you will find that management philosophies can change on a dime.

Take a walk in the business book section of Borders (I guess you already have if you purchased this book—though I hoped it would be on the *New York Times* bestsellers table), and you will see that books on management philosophy are big business. The reason is that management is a very difficult thing. Scores of new titles each week promise to offer some new style and strategy. While these books can be useful, few offer long-term answers to management issues, most of which any good management team should already know.

Are You Fad Surfing?

Addiction to fad surfing can really hurt a company. There's something to be said for consistency, even if you're not doing the perfect job. Here's a list of some popular management styles:

Day-care style: If you treat employees like toddlers, be ready to change their diapers.

Machiavelli style: Better that they fear you than love you.

Spanish Inquisition style: It works, but it's highly illegal.

Buddy style: Be their best buddy—until it's time to make cuts.

Jewish grandmother style: Guilt goes a long way in keeping your workers in line.

Google style: Give them free food and free dry cleaning and they'll never leave you.

Stalin style: Get rid of key players to rid yourself of rivals and establish your power base.

British colonial style: Staff jobs with natives except for top managers. Enforce policy with a whip.

The plague style: Get rid of 30 percent of your workforce at random, just to keep them on their toes.

Frat-boy style: Instead of casual Friday, hold keg Friday, complete with strippers, togas, and beer bongs.

➕ **FIRST COINED:** George Harris, "Fad-Surfers, Risk-Dodgers, and Beloved Companies," *Harvard Business Review,* February 1993.

FALLEN ANGEL

The Devil Made Me Do It

{ **WHAT IT MEANS:** A stock that has fallen significantly from its all-time high

While it would be nice to blame very bad investment decisions on the most famous fallen angel, named Lucifer (or "Lucy," if you're on a familiar basis), sometimes you've just got to take the rap yourself. Then again, fallen angels can be awful tricky.

In the financial world, fallen angels are stocks that have fallen from the heavens and now trade at earthy, perhaps even subterranean levels. Unlike the fallen angels of the biblical sort, however, these stocks haven't been banished from the heavens and may even return. To determine which fallen angels are promising, investors usually look for stocks that have dropped based on the market's overreaction to negative news. So, if a company's earnings are lower than expected, the stock usually drops a little. However, if the market overreacts and the stock falls to the floor, this stock just might be a fallen angel you want to keep your eye on.

For some help picking which fallen angels are going to rise back toward the sky and which ones have broken wings, you can tune in to TV's *Mad Money* with investment guru Jim Cramer. He often points out these angelic opportunities.

➕ **FIRST COINED:** L. O. Hooper, "The Public Takes Over," *Forbes,* February 1976.

FEATHERBEDDING

We're Light As a Feather

Bosses always seem to kvetch that productivity is lower than it should be, as if there were some con-

{ **WHAT IT MEANS:**
Limiting productivity in order to require more employees than necessary

spiracy ensuring that the level of output didn't exceed a given amount. While this is usually pure paranoia, in the case of featherbedding, it's actually true.

The term *featherbedding* is most often associated with labor union practices in the United States. Some unions, fearing to lose jobs to some technological or other advance, insist on purposely inefficient work rules, so that more workers will be needed to do the job.

Conspiracy or Stupidity?

Sometimes, it's hard to tell whether there is featherbedding going on or just plain silliness. If you're an employer, however, be on the lookout for both.

- **Conspiracy:** Your employees all take water breaks at the same time, forming a long but orderly single-file line.
- **Stupidity:** You find your employees bathing and frolicking at the water cooler.
- **Conspiracy:** When you disagree with employees, you overhear words like *strike, scab,* and *capitalist pig.*
- **Stupidity:** When you disagree with employees, you overhear words like *poopyhead, meanie,* or *You make me sad.*
- **Conspiracy:** Employees all report to the doctor on the same day.
- **Stupidity:** Employees all report to the doctor on the same day after slipping and falling during water-cooler revelries.

FEEBATE

Feedom from Oil Dependency

WHAT IT MEANS: A government program that charges fees on fuel-inefficient vehicles and offers rebates on fuel-efficient vehicles

For years, many have championed the feebate as a partial solution to environmental problems caused by cars. But the car feebate never really got off the ground. Now that the fossil-fuel debate has, once again, a saleable aspect to conservatives as well as conservationists—all that foreign oil, national security jazz—we might see feebate schemes begin to take hold.

If feebates were implemented, when you bought a new car, you would pay an extra fee if it were a gas guzzler or get a rebate if it were a hybrid. A neutral point would be set so that fees and rebates balanced. So it would not be either an inflationary measure or a tax. Similar plans have been proposed to reduce the consumption of water and other resources.

WORST FEEBATE SCHEMES

- Tax young prostitutes and subsidize the older ones to level the playing field.
- Tax vowels and subsidize consonants to promote letter-usage equality.
- Tax overweight people and subsidize the thin to help fight obesity.

➕ **FIRST COINED:** Amory B. Lovins and L. Hunter Lovins, "Make Fuel Efficiency Our Gulf Strategy," *New York Times,* December 1990.

FICTOMERCIAL

Do Ads Imitate Art, or Does Art Imitate Ads?

WHAT IT MEANS:
A work of fiction written in order to promote or advertise a product or service

The new era of advertising is here. It's called the fictomercial, which is essentially a commercial wrapped up in a work of fiction such as a novel. Now a $2 billion business and growing fast, advertisers are increasingly turning to this nontraditional form of product promotion. After all, how else can you reach a potential customer nowadays with TiVo?

Biz fact: One popular fictomercial is Mark Haskell Smith's cool Lexus comic entitled "Black Sapphire Pearl," which is featured on the Lexus Web site and in Lexus's quarterly magazine.

Upcoming Fictomercials

The Unbearable Lightness of Bud Light: A novel about love, the Cold War, and good ol' American beer.

Waiting for Gucci: A play about two unfashionable middle-aged women waiting for something or someone named Gucci to change their lives—and their shoes.

The Da Vinci Coke: A mystery about a chemistry professor whose research takes him to the Vatican, where he believes the original, thousand-year-old Coca Cola formulation is hidden under the floor of the Sistine Chapel.

War and Pizza Hut: An epic novel set in the times of Napoleonic Russia, where, after running out of beets to make borscht, the heroic Russian peasantry reluctantly turn to an unlikely source of sustenance—Pizza Hut.

✚ **FIRST COINED**: Sylvia Brownrigg, "Your Ad Here," *New York Times,* November 2001.

FINANCIAL PARENTING

Don't Turn Your Kids into Richie Rich

WHAT IT MEANS: Educational services for the children of wealthy parents

Sudden wealth is a blessing. It allows people to buy things they've always wanted, live in their dream house, and take lavish vacations all over the world. But sudden wealth also brings with it some anxiety, particularly when it comes to raising kids. While any loving parent with cash wants to buy their kid everything he or she wants, some parents fear that growing up with a lot of money will turn their little ones into spoiled brats.

To make sure their kids don't grow up to be mediocre students who fail miserably at every business they attempt (think George W. Bush), some parents are taking advantage of so-called financial parenting services, designed to help the family deal with all this money.

Poor, poor rich people.

ARE YOUR KIDS TOO SPOILED?

- They have their assistant write their Christmas list.
- They have a plasma TV in their bedroom.
- When you asked them what they wanted for their birthday they said, "Hawaii."
- When you told them they were grounded, they thought it meant they couldn't use the family jet.
- On a camping trip, they brought their bodyguard to protect against bear attacks.
- Their favorite food is sushi.
- They're sick and tired of having to get "all dressed up" for dinner at the White House.
- They asked to see a shrink because of "classwork-related stress."
- They love the opera (and they're not gay or Italian).
- Their favorite sport is polo.

FINANCIAL PORNOGRAPHY

You Scratch My Back and I'll . . .

There have always been favors in business. A quid pro quo kind of thing. But when the promotion of a person or a product puts inves-

WHAT IT MEANS:

Books, newsletters, and articles that glorify financiers, money managers, and the deals they make

tors at risk, you've got to make sure that you have protection—in the form of good old-fashioned objective journalism, that is.

Unlike other kinds of porno, financial smut contains no nudity, and even those that produce it wouldn't try and pass it off as art. And if you've ever taken a look at the CEO-of-the-month centerfold, you'll never get off again. Unless, of course, you have a thing for bald, middle-aged, overweight, pock-marked, alcoholic divorcees. And the men are even less attractive!

✚ **FIRST COINED:** Bruce Ingersoll, "Regulating Advice," *Wall Street Journal*, November 1984.

FLIGHT TO QUALITY

Shakin' in Your Boots

The flight to quality is usually caused by one of two things: If

> **WHAT IT MEANS:**
> The flow of money from riskier investments to safer ones

there is uncertainty or fear in the financial markets, investors may move their money out of equities and into government securities and money market funds. Or if there is political turmoil in the air and fear in international markets, investors may move their money from high-risk countries with political unrest and volatile economic conditions to the less risky countries.

Stocks and Bonds

One good indication of a flight to quality is a dramatic fall of the yield on government securities, the classic safe investment, as a result of the increased demand for them. The market adjusts returns so that safe investments pay less than risky ones. Much less. On average, stocks have returned about 12 percent per year over the last fifty years, while cash accounts and bonds have run around 6 percent. While stocks outperform cash accounts and bonds, they only do so over the long term. Any one year might drown an investor in red ink. Mark Twain once said, "October is one of the peculiarly dangerous months to speculate in stocks. Others are July, January, April, September, November, May, March, June, December, August, and February."

FRAZZING

Don't Be a Sucker!

WHAT IT MEANS:
Frantic, ineffective multitasking

It's 9 A.M. when you get to work. After exchanging an exhausting amount of "good mornings" and "hellos" to your colleagues, you make your way to your desk, sit down, and turn on the computer. First stop: your e-mail inbox.

Though it sounds tedious, you can find out a lot of interesting things while sifting through your e-mails, such as exciting stocks that are "ready to explode," new ways to fix your credit, and "amazing" deals on all sorts of products and services, especially from PayPal.

What's more, you can find out a lot about yourself. You might learn that you have an abnormally small penis (particularly alarming if you're a woman) or that you are overweight and in dire need of some new weight-loss medication. But it's not all bad news. Despite your physical shortcomings, you'll no doubt smile when you read about your incredible chance to make millions by just sending a small amount of money to a Nigerian account. Don't worry, these political prisoners just need a bank account to hide their fortune in—you can trust them. And, if this weren't exciting enough, you might find out that you have won yet another European lottery. Yes, though it might seem suspicious since you live in Jersey, don't worry—just send your bank info to the address and they'll transfer your winnings in no time. But before you do, check your watch; thirty minutes have already been squandered and the real frazzing hasn't even begun.

Fighting Frazzing

Now that you've finished searching though your e-mails, you'll no doubt go on the Net for "just a second" and wind up wasting another hour. And even if you do start that important project, between all the e-mails, the phone calls (both in the office and on your cell), and even more e-mails on your Blackberry, the chances of you finishing it quickly are slim to none. Yes, the very technology that's supposedly making you faster and more productive is actually slowing you down. In fact, according to *Time* magazine, frazzing and SCREENSUCKING cost the American economy over $588 billion each year.

FRUGGING

Frug Off

The only thing more annoying than being solicited to participate in a survey is being solicited to partici-

WHAT IT MEANS:
Soliciting a donation while pretending to conduct market research

pate in a fake one. An acronym for "fund-raising under the guise of research," *frugging* occurs when a product marketer pretends to be a market researcher conducting a statistical survey, when in fact he or she is just trying to get your money. So, if you get a call and a company asks you if you would like to participate in their survey, make sure to ask them who they are and what they are surveying. If they call you around dinner time, don't investigate any further—just tell them to frug off.

GADGET PORN

Me So Techie

There was a time, not so long ago, that only doctors and drug dealers

WHAT IT MEANS:
Advertising that glorifies high-tech devices

carried pagers. These days, of course, it's a little different. Gadget porn has us all coveting Blackberries, Razr phones, iPods, and the like.

iSuck

Consider an iPod commercial. A woman dancing alone with headphones plugged into her brain. "Wow," you think, "wouldn't it be wildly cool if I could wear headphones and dance by myself?" You can! Your pre-iPod MP3 player, your Walkman, and your Discman are all sitting in a box somewhere. Your iPod will soon join them.

BEST GADGET COMMERCIAL
- **Red iPod . . .** A portion of the profits go to fight AIDS. Helping humanity is easier when you get something tangible out of it.
- **PC versus Mac . . .** Mac users are hipper, but who has more money? Especially after buying a MacBook.
- **Gateway . . .** Now every time you drive by a dairy farm, you'll think about buying a new Gateway.

➕ **FIRST COINED:** R. U. Sirius, "The Road Behind," *Artforum,* April 1, 1996.

GARBATRAGE

Takeover Frenzy!

{**WHAT IT MEANS:**

Companies that are overvalued by investors because of a recent takeover in their industry

Many investors feel that one initial takeover is a precursor to more takeovers within the sector. While this could be true, it's likely speculation, and these stocks probably have no real reason to rise. Those who believe in behavioral finance theory would view the garbatrage phenomenon as evidence that supports their theory. See FLIGHT TO QUALITY and HERD INVESTMENT.

G

Garbage + Arbitrage

This portmanteau word is derived from the words *garbage* and *arbitrage*. In case you're unfamiliar with arbitrage, it's the practice of taking advantage of a price difference between two markets. So, if you can buy bubble gum in Los Angeles for two cents a stick and sell it in New York for three cents a stick, you're an arbitrageur. If you can do this enough, the price gap will disappear and you will make a hefty profit.

Similarly, in garbatrage, the supposedly "underpriced" stock is bought in the equity markets and is expected to be sold privately to a buyout firm, which would pay a premium for the shares. But since this won't likely happen, the companies turn out to be overvalued, hence garbatrage.

And garbage, as my wife points out, is piling up in our kitchen. In a minute, honey, I promise.

> "My wife is always trying to get rid of me. The other day she told me to put the garbage out. I said to her I already did. She told me to go and keep an eye on it."
>
> *Rodney Dangerfield*

GATOR

Highjackware!

WHAT IT MEANS: Spyware that displays a company's ad on a rival's Web site

The term *gator* is named after the Gator Corporation (now called the Claria Corporation), a spyware company. The name change was probably due to, in part, an attempt by the company to distance itself from the reputation it had earned from its products.

The gator program was installed together with free programs, such as games and p2p file-sharing programs. In the past, it had been installed through misleading or surreptitious means, usually without disclosing that it would be monitoring Web-browsing habits and displaying ads based on user profiles.

Alligators in Cyberspace

In the past, Gator undercut many Internet publishers by replacing banner ads on Web sites with its own, a practice also known as gatoring. By doing this, Gator made advertising content by other Web sites impotent to bring in customers and may have deprived Web sites of revenue.

In 2002, many large publishers, including the *New York Post*, the *New York Times*, and Dow Jones & Company, sued Gator for its practice of replacing ads. Most of the lawsuits were settled out of court.

Though its products were universally recognized as spyware, the company denies it and has attempted to suppress such labels with litigation. In September 2003, the company started threatening Web sites that identified Gator as spyware with libel lawsuits.

Reformgation

Today the Claria Corporation describes itself by saying:

> *Claria Corporation helps business partners engage with their consumers by providing a personalization platform that powers Web sites, software applications, and hardware devices. This market-proven personalization technology gives consumers a more relevant, engaging and simplified Internet experience.*

Whatever, gatorers.

GAZUMP

- -

Oy Gezump

Supposedly derived from the Yiddish word *gezumph*, meaning
to cheat or overcharge, *gazump*

became widely used in England in the 1920s to refer to any kind
of swindle. Today, the term is reserved for a real estate transac-
tion in which the price of a property is raised just before the
papers are signed and the deal is done.

There are many tricks to any trade, and real estate is no
different. Agents and property owners use all sorts of unscrupulous tactics to persuade you to pay more than originally
agreed, including lying about a higher offer from another buyer.
Gazumping is more of a problem in England than in the United
States, where verbal agreements, though hard to prove, can be
legally binding.

While gazumping is naturally more popular in a seller's market when the real estate prices are high (otherwise the victim
buyer would just walk away from the deal), the opposite tactic,
gazunder, sometimes occurs in a buyer's market. This is when
a buyer suddenly drops his offer before the deal is signed in
the hope that the seller will be bullied into accepting the lower
offer.

GEEKSTA RAP

- -

Geeksta's Paradise

At first glance, Silicon Valley might
not seem like a rough town. Rarely
are there drive-by shootings, and

even a bar fight is usually broken up by the French waitstaff.

But not all geeks are wimps. Just because you graduated summa cum laude with a computer science degree, wear your pants pulled up as high as your nipples, and of course, you still rock the pocket protector (but it does make good sense if you want to avoid getting ink on your shirt), that doesn't mean that you can't be as slick as the next cat.

Rajeev Bajaj, a Silicon Valley entrepreneur, is an example of the hipper side of Silicon Valley. The original geeksta, his *Geek Rhythms* debut album includes lyrics about things like electrons, software, and rebooting.

Biz Rap

Two can play at that game. I'll battle these geeks any day.

> *Chillin' with the homies in the board room*
> *Scheming on a way to make our stock boom*
> *Sellin' my shares to buy a new SUV*
> *I hopes I don't get indicted by the SEC*

> *But if I do*
> *It'll be aiight*
> *Cause I gots the lawyers to put up a fight*

✚ **FIRST COINED**: Alex Cruden, "Five Things About Geeksta Rap," *Detroit Free Press*, December 2006.

GHOST WORK

Operation Apparition

All across America, offices are haunted by the ghosts of former employees. But forget about trying

WHAT IT MEANS:
Work that used to be done by recently fired employees, now handled by the remaining staff

to capture these apparitions with a camera and sell them to Ripley's Believe It or Not. These ghouls remain unseen. They do, unfortunately, leave their work behind for you and the remaining staff to make up. Sometimes, this can mean so much extra work that you might actually wish you were a ghost, too.

➕ **FIRST COINED:** This sense of the phrase was coined by management consultant Hamilton Beazley in his 2002 book, *Continuity Management.* Other, older uses of *ghost work* include work billed for but not performed and work completed during the graveyard shift.

GODFATHER OFFER

An Offer You Can't Refuse

When Marlon Brando famously uttered, "I'm going to make him an offer he can't refuse" in *The Godfather,* movie history was made. Even more memorable was when he showed that he wasn't kidding.

WHAT IT MEANS:
An irrefutable takeover offer made to a target company by an acquiring company

A godfather offer, however, probably won't involve decapitating horses as a way of negotiating, nor does it have to be made while stroking a cat or wearing a tux. Instead, in a far less dramatic but far more professional manner, the godfather offer is usually extremely generous, making it very hard for the target company to say no. If the company does refuse, shareholders might file a lawsuit against the management in an act of rebellion. But that's probably as far as they'll take it—unless, of course, they're shareholders in Murder, Inc.

G

GOLDEN HANDCUFFS

Should I Stay or Should I Go Now?

The result of a key employee leaving can be a devastating setback for even a large company. This is

particularly the case in the brokerage business, where the threat of a broker taking clients with him or her to a new firm is cause for concern. To keep these employees off Monster.com and on task, companies attempt to handcuff these golden employees by offering them significant benefits if they stick around.

Though certainly appreciated, raising an employee's salary isn't an example of a golden handcuff. After all, paying them today could still lead them to leave tomorrow. Nope, to get someone to stay when they're inclined to leave requires a little more ingenuity. Slapping on the golden handcuffs is an artful business. You've got to keep those employees hanging on the promise of future rewards, but not too far in the future—or else they might not stay engaged. Some of the most shimmering golden handcuffs are stock options that can't be sold for a certain amount of time, bonuses that aren't payable right away, and promises of more interesting projects.

Most Hare-Brained Golden Handcuff Schemes

After handing in your letter of resignation, your boss tries to persuade you to reconsider by:

- Offering options that come to term in nine years.
- Promising an unlimited lifetime supply of sticky notes.
- Building you a bigger office in the basement.

G

- Pledging to donate her kidney to you if it is ever needed.
- Offering his daughter's hand in marriage.

GOOGLE BOMBING

Gaga for Google

WHAT IT MEANS:

Attempting to influence the ranking order of a Web page in the search results returned by Google

Most everyone by now has used the word *Google* as a verb. Not since Xerox has a trademarked name of a product become so adopted by the public for generic use (though, as evidenced by a statement to the media in 2006, Google would rather it wasn't). But there are other neologisms that have been spawned by the goliath search engine, such as *Google bombing* (also, *Google washing*). Here's how it works.

When you are Googling for a certain page, Google's PageRank algorithm will rank a page higher if sites that link to that page all use consistent anchor text (the visible text in a link). This means that when you Google *moron,* for example, if enough people have used that word in their anchor text linking to your page, your name will show up on Google's search results first! (Even if you are not the self-deprecating type and never refer to yourself on your homepage as a moron.) When this happens, you know you've been Google bombed.

Google bombing was first coined on April 6, 2001, in an article by Adam Mathes. Mathes became aware of Google bombing after noticing that a Google search for *Internet rockstar* brought up Ben Brown as the first result, even though the words didn't appear on Brown's page. He reckoned that Google must have returned Brown as the first result because Brown's fans must have used that phrase on their own pages. Like any good pal, he tested his theory by trying to have his friend Andy Pressman come up as the first result in a query for *talentless hack*. He succeeded. Ironically, in 2004, Mathes's own site met the same fate.

Despite the successful Google bombing of Microsoft in 1998 (the company came up first in a search for *More evil than Satan!*), Google bombs have a limited effect on businesses due to their short life span. (Many people hear about them quickly.) It is for this reason that few companies are worried about the negative impact of Google bombing.

More effective at poking fun at political figures, a sizeable amount of Google bombing is politically motivated. For example, on June 1, 2000, a search for *miserable failure* brought up the official biography of George W. Bush as the first Google result. Not limited to Google, the Google bomb brought up the site as number one on Yahoo! and MSN and number two on Ask Jeeves.

If you think you have what it takes to be a great Google bomber, drop bombs with the best of them the next time there is a Google bombing competition. Yes, you heard me right. Where? Don't ask me. Google it!

GRASS CEILING

Sexism: Par for the Course

WHAT IT MEANS:
A set of social barriers that prevents or discourages women from playing golf to conduct business

Like the ever-so-visible glass ceiling, the grass ceiling can also prevent women from soaring to the top of the corporate world. By thwarting women from joining prestigious country clubs, sexist members of the old boys' network are thwarting their ability to succeed in business as well.

Golf is big business. Not just in terms of the amount of money Tiger Woods rakes in each year, or the cost of playing golf (even miniature golf is a ripoff), but also in terms of the number of business deals that are struck on the course. Because it's a great place to network and make important contacts, membership in a country club can mean the difference between hitting a hole-in-one and playing caddy.

OTHER PLACES WOMEN USUALLY MISS OUT ON BUSINESS DEALS

- The men's locker room
- The sauna at the health club
- The strip club
- Fishing and hunting trips
- Saudi Arabia (they can go, but they have to keep quiet)

➕ **FIRST COINED:** Carolyn Pione, Associated Press, May 1994.

GRAY MATTER

It's Good to Be Gray

WHAT IT MEANS: Older, experienced executives hired by startup firms in an effort to make the company look more established

Today's young, energetic entrepreneurs have everything they need to succeed—they've got the capital, they've got the brains, and they've got the connections. But there's one thing that these kids didn't learn in business school or in computer class that they'll need to go all the way—a little thing called experience. At least, that's how the market sometimes sees it. And that's why smart young businesspeople with startups look to the older generation to provide the credibility their company needs to make it.

When It's Time to Go Gray

Here are some tips that your young company needs some gray matter:

- The company president just recently got the right to vote.
- Every time there's a birthday party, someone complains that the clown "scared me."
- At the Christmas party, there were complaints that Santa showed up in a cab not pulled by reindeer.
- When you tell a coworker you were in 'Nam, they ask you where you stayed.
- The CFO rides a skateboard to work.
- The most popular topic of conversation at the water cooler is dinosaurs.
- The office was redesigned because of complaints of "monsters in the closets."
- The corporate motto is "I love you, you love me, we're a happy company."
- Happy hour is spent at Chuck E. Cheese.
- The cafeteria serves only peanut-butter-and-jelly sandwiches or Sloppy Joes.

GUN JUMPING

Don't Jump the Gun

Named for the racing phrase that means a runner has started before the starter pistol has been fired,

WHAT IT MEANS:
Trading on information that has yet to be revealed to the public

gun jumping in finance can also be a disqualifying offense. Let's say you know something about a company that hasn't yet been made public. This gives you an edge over every other investor in the world. This informational asymmetry is illegal to act upon, but people still do because it's hard to prove.

Now if a CEO or the CFO acts upon such information, it's pretty easy to see. Their trading is much more public than others,

G

and they would get busted. Their brother, their friend, and their mom, however, could make a nice little wad of cash pretty easily, if they knew. And while the information is less reliable the further you are from the original source, so is any connection to it. At some point, this information is spread around the world and is probably either old or inaccurate. Then your poker buddies tell you about it.

GUNSLINGER

Hedge-Fund Cowboys

If you've ever been to Wall Street, don't let the skyscrapers and the suits fool you. There may be no

WHAT IT MEANS:

A high-strung portfolio manager who favors very high-risk, high-return investments

horses, no brothels (well, not conspicuous ones anyway), and no gunfights with the local sheriff—but that don't mean it ain't a battle zone. Wall Street is teeming with gunslingers who will risk everything to be the top gun in town. Among the wildest of these cowboys are hedge-fund managers, a notoriously brazen bunch.

What Are Hedge Funds?

Hedge funds are private pools of capital that employ hedging techniques such as short selling, use of options and futures, market arbitrage (the simultaneous purchase and sale of the same security in different markets), the use of leverage, and investing in risky markets. These strategies are designed to hedge against inferior returns, providing exceptional returns in both bull and bear markets. Sometimes these strategies work, sometimes they don't. What's more, increased competition has made hedge-fund investing increasingly risky.

G

For example, consider the infamous implosion of hedge fund Aramanth Advisors, LLC, which sent shockwaves throughout the financial world. Led by thirty-two-year-old hedge-fund cowboy Brian Hunter, the fund roped in phenomenal returns for its first eighteen months. Betting on the right side of gas prices when Hurricane Katrina caused them to spike, he racked up huge gains in its portfolio, attracting a host of new investors. Unfortunately, however, the following summer this Hunter tried it again, only to come home empty-handed after a horrendous hurricane season failed to develop. This bet on natural-gas futures destroyed Aramanth, causing an estimated $6.6 billion loss in a $9 billion portfolio.

However, just because investors in Aramanth didn't ride off into the sunset doesn't mean that other hedge funds don't do extraordinarily well. In fact, some of the best-performing funds can lasso in annual gains of 200 to 300 percent.

Note: Hedge fund investing is limited to "accredited investors," individuals with net worth of $2.5 million (excluding the home) with an annual income of $200,000 for the last two years or a joint income of $300,000, as well as a "reasonable expectation" that this will continue.

Is Your Portfolio Manager a Gunslinger?

While hedge-fund managers might be the most untamed cowboys on Wall Street, any money manager can be a gunslinger. Here are some signs that your investment cowboy has become an investment outlaw:

- She tells you to buy Ford stock.
- He refers to the SEC as the "the law."
- She suggests you buy Mexican American war bonds.
- He prefers pink sheet–listed stocks.
- She's trying to organize a buyout of Wal-Mart.

G

HEDONIC TREADMILL

Money Doesn't Buy Happiness

We've all heard the cliché over and over again—but that doesn't mean it isn't true. It is. Just think about the last raise that you had been waiting

for and finally received. Did you jump for joy? Sure, but fast forward a week, and you were bitching about something new.

In fact, some progressive anthropologists believe that what really separates humans from animals is not the ability to plan for the future, make moral choices, or believe in a creator, but the ability to kvetch no matter how good things seem to get.

However, the hedonic treadmill theory doesn't claim that there are no happy people, just that happiness comes mostly from within, a result of your genetics, not your paycheck.

Get off the Treadmill

While running on the hedonic treadmill may be frustrating and frivolous, some worldly pleasures do, at least, provide some temporary relief. Here are some things you can always try to cheer you up:

For Men	For Women
Go fishing	Get a facial
Have sex	Buy shoes
Kill things	Watch *Oprah*
Drink a beer	Gossip
Scratch yourself	Get your nails done
Masturbate	Go out dancing
Have more sex	Buy more shoes
Work on your car	Eat a salad
Masturbate again	Buy more shoes
Smoke a cigar	Refuse to conform to basic traffic rules

➕ **FIRST COINED:** T. Lott, "Happiness: Three Academics Look for Life's Biggest Secret," *Sunday Herald,* April 1990.

HERD INVESTMENT

Old MacDonald Had a Fund

Herd investment has nothing to do with investing in cows, farms, or even dairy products. Though, if you wanted to buy a cow, a few thousand dollars would be enough for a really nice one.

WHAT IT MEANS:

An investment based on what other people or institutions are investing in rather than on analysis

Investment Lemmings

There are times, despite our big brains, that we behave like little rodents. As the saying goes, we follow the herd. Sometimes it makes sense; sometimes it doesn't. If you want to play it relatively safe, why not invest in the S&P Index like everyone else? But if you're buying Stockbomb.com just because your drinking buddies have, don't expect to see your money ever again.

The same can be true for trading on news. Once the news is released, the market responds immediately. Unless you're watching for press releases all day long, and even then, you're not going to beat the pros.

Warren Buffett put it this way: "Most people get interested in stocks when everyone else is. The time to get interested is when no one else is. You can't buy what is popular and do well."

Groupthink

Herd investment is a type of metal phenomenon similar to groupthink, where members of a group minimize conflict and reach consensus without testing, analyzing, or evaluating ideas. In groupthink, group members avoid promoting viewpoints outside the comfort zone of consensus thinking. Basically, when all your buddies are saying Stockbomb.com is the best company in the world, don't just accept it; do a little research yourself.

Truth is, it's tough to think for yourself when your instincts are telling you that the safe thing is to do what everyone else is doing. But this isn't really a safer thing is to do. It just makes you feel a little less like a moron when things go badly.

> "Men, it has been well said, think in herds; it will be seen that they go mad in herds, while they only recover their senses slowly, and one by one."
>
> *Charles Mackay*

> "The herd instinct among forecasters makes sheep look like independent thinkers."
>
> *Edgar R. Fiedler*

> "The herd instinct seems to be the strongest human emotion, one that the race is constantly breeding off as the mavericks are liquidated. Happiness is running with the crowd."
>
> *John Train*

➕ **FIRST COINED:** Jim Hoagland, "Asia—One for the Wizards," *Washington Post.*

HOSTILE TAKEOVER

Not Your Friendly Takeover

Once the scourge of the business world, hostile takeovers are now seen in more neutral terms. While

{ WHAT IT MEANS:
A takeover attempt that is stalwartly resisted by the target firm

employee morale of the target firm can quickly turn to animosity against the acquiring firm, this is not always the case. And, investors can see the buyout as a blessing for the long-term health of the company.

Hostile takeovers are takeover attempts that are resisted by the target firm. A hostile takeover allows a suitor to bypass management. This allows the target company's shareholders to choose to sell or hold.

A Nicer, Friendlier Takeover

Friendly takeovers, on the other hand, are when a target company's board of directors agrees to a merger. In a friendly takeover, a public offer of stock or cash is made by the acquiring firm, and the board of the target firm will publicly approve the buyout terms, which may still require shareholder or regulatory approval.

Enter the Barbarians

The most famous and, until recently, the largest buyout ever was the Kohlberg Kravis Roberts & Co. takeover of RJR Nabisco in 1989. The $25 billion takeover of RJR Nabisco was financed with $1.5 billion in equity and a complex mixture of bank debt, bonds, and preferred stock. Sometimes it pays to have good credit.

HUNDRED-HUNDRED SPLIT

Giving 200 Percent

WHAT IT MEANS:
Having two managers, each of whom wants 100 percent of your time

Who is the arbiter of your time? If both managers think it's them, it's time to pit them against each other. It may not help, but it will sure be fun. Here are some things to try:

1. Send Valentine's Day cards to Boss A's spouse from Boss B.
2. Boss A likes pizza. Put a slice on Boss B's chair.
3. Send an anonymous note to Boss C (the big boss) that Boss B and Boss A are embezzling funds. That should keep them off your back for a while.
4. Kidnap Boss A's cat and sign the ransom note "Boss B."
5. On Boss B's birthday, send a stripper to the house during family dinner time. Compliments of Boss A, of course.

➕ **FIRST COINED:** DangerousLogic (*www.dangerouslogic.com*), October 2005.

HYPE CYCLE

The Cycle of Life

WHAT IT MEANS:
A detailed representation of a product's movement from development to commercialization

The business world and the animal kingdom have a lot in common. They're both brutal, they're both unpredictable, and in both it's the strong that survive. But despite hard times, the birth of new life is a cause for celebration.

In business, this new life takes the form of a new technology or product whose parent company believes has great potential for success. But sometimes you can't really rely on what parents have to say about their offspring—even if most end up a disappointment. After all, no matter how unattractive or useless the product might be, it's only natural for a company to have trouble admitting it. That's why Gartner, Inc., an objective information and technology research and advisory firm, developed the "hype cycle" in 1995.

Ganter's hype cycle charts the overexcitement and subsequent disappointment that often occurs after a new technology is introduced. In addition, it also illustrates how and when technologies become widely accepted. Hype cycles aim to separate the hype from the reality, and enable CEOs to decide whether or not a particular technology is ready for market.

Five Easy Phases

Gartner's hype cycle is a five-part sequence:

1. **Technology trigger:** A breakthrough that generates considerable interest.
2. **Peak of inflated expectations:** Tales of the technology's successes cause a flurry of hype, while the technology's failures and setbacks are ignored.
3. **Trough of disillusionment:** Unable to live up to the overinflated expectations, the technology becomes unfashionable and the press abandons it.
4. **Slope of enlightenment:** Though out of the spotlight, experimentation continues, leading to a better understanding of the technology's risks and benefits.
5. **Plateau of productivity:** The actual benefits of the technology are demonstrated and accepted. Second- and third-generation versions make it increasingly stable. The plateau varies according to whether the technology is broadly applicable or benefits only a niche market.

INCONSPICUOUS CONSUMPTION

The Theory of the Working Class

WHAT IT MEANS:

Buying things that are indicative of being of a lower socioeconomic class

The term *inconspicuous consumption* is a play on *conspicuous consumption,* a term first coined by Thorstein Veblen in his famous book, *Theory of the Leisure Class:*

> *Conspicuous consumption of valuable goods is a means of reputability to the gentleman of leisure. As wealth accumulates on his hands, his own unaided effort will not avail to sufficiently put his opulence in evidence by this method. The aid of friends and competitors is therefore brought in by resorting to the giving of valuable presents and expensive feasts and entertainments.*

Thus, conspicuous consumers spend money to impress others and to make sure that everyone knows that they're big shots. Inconspicuous consumers, on the other hand, don't want to impress anyone. In fact, what they really want is for everyone to think that they are poorer than they really are.

Conspicuous	Less Conspicuous	Inconspicuous
Mercedes Benz	Volvo	Huffy
filet mignon	New York strip	BK Broiler
Prada	Gap	Salvation Army
MacBook	Dell	library card
Hilton	Holiday Inn	Motel 6
Rolex	Timex	the sun
iPod	Discman	humming
platinum ring	gold ring	paper clip

✚ **FIRST COINED:** Connie Cutter, "I'm O.K.—You're Fat," *Sojourner: The Women's Forum,* April 1980.

INSIDER NON-TRADING

Inacting Up

In the financial world, information is power. Knowing what the other guy doesn't has turned many unscrupulous sharks into gazillionaires. But it's also highly illegal to buy or sell a stock because you know something that the public doesn't. It's called insider trading, and it could get you into a lot of trouble. Think Martha Stewart.

Yet, what about deciding *not* to buy or sell a stock based on insider information?

Here's a scenario: An executive at Company A learns in a board meeting that the firm's lead drug product to treat toenail fungus has just been approved by the FDA. This is big news, and when it's announced, the company's shares will no doubt soar. If the executive immediately goes into her office and buys a bunch of stock, she's obviously guilty of insider trading. But what if, because of the announcement, she chooses not to *sell* when she had previously planned to?

This action, or rather *lack* of action based on insider information, happens more than you might think. In fact, many experts in securities regulation consider it a very serious problem.

➕ **FIRST COINED:** William A. Kelly Jr., "The Plague of Insider Non-Trading," *Wall Street Journal*, December 1986.

INTERSOURCE

Let's Get It On

Anyone who's ever called Microsoft for software assistance knows that companies are increasingly outsourcing jobs overseas. In fact, *outsourcing* has become a household word over the past few years. It affects everyone, from automobile workers in Detroit to IT specialists in Silicon Valley. However, while outsourcing can increase the bottom line, it can also create kinks in the supply chain. That's why many companies are now opting to intersource their jobs. By intersourcing, these companies can build a stronger and more intimate bond with the outside firm or manufacturer to whom they ship their jobs.

How to Intersource Safely

Let's face it, intersourcing is fun—especially for stressed-out CEOs looking to save on labor costs. But like any operation, it can also be a bit risky. Here's a list of things to watch out for to ensure that your experience during intersourcing goes as smoothly and safely as possible:

- Know your intersource partner. Find out what they need to perform at peak levels.
- Check your partner's history. Find out who they've worked with in the past. Remember, that you're not only having intersource with them, you're having intersource with everyone they've worked with, too.
- Make sure it's a good fit. Don't force it.
- If you are having trouble making it work, talk to your partner about how to improve your intersource. If that doesn't work, just think about baseball. If this doesn't help, hire some outside consultants to monitor and analyze the operation.
- Even a smooth and profitable partnership can become dull after a while. To spice things up, add another intersource partner to the boardroom. But beware, three-way intersourcing, while certainly fun, can become a source of jealousy.

JACKPOT JUSTICE

Casino Royale

We know about lawsuits in the United States. We have the most litigious society on Earth, and

WHAT IT MEANS:

Awarding huge monetary settlements to plaintiffs in court cases

by far the most lawyers. While this can mean big bucks for those that sue and big bucks for the attorneys who represent them, it can also turn the business world upside down, creating insanely high insurance costs that would send shivers down any employer's spine. Fear of worker's compensation suits, sexual harassment suits, or discrimination suits can turn even the most optimistic and trusting executive into a suspicious paranoid. Of course, all this legal activity does create one undeniable net benefit for all of us: hundreds of really, really good lawyer jokes.

Best Lawyer Jokes

Everyone has a favorite. Here are a few of ours:

Q: What do you call a million lawyers at the bottom of the sea?
A: A good start.

Q: What do you throw to a drowning lawyer?
A: His partners.

Q: How can you tell when a lawyer is lying?
A: His lips are moving.

Q: How do you get a group of lawyers to smile for a photo?
A: Just say, "Fees!"

Q: How many lawyer jokes are there?
A: Only three. The rest are true stories.

A Reasonable Fee

A man calls a lawyer and asks, "How much would you charge for just answering three simple questions?"

The lawyer replies, "A thousand dollars."

"A thousand dollars!" exclaims the man. "That's very expensive, isn't it?"

"It certainly is," says the lawyer. "Now, what's your third question?"

➕ **FIRST COINED:** Glen Elsasser, "Ballots Reflecting Insurance Revolt Proposals Unlikely to Stop Movement," *Chicago Tribune,* October 1986.

JEKYLL AND HYDE

WHAT IT MEANS:

The strengths and weaknesses of a company's financial statements

Man and Monster

As R. L. Stevenson's *The Strange Case of Dr. Jekyll and Mr. Hyde* gruesomely illustrates, life is full of contradictions and divisions. Whether it's between id and superego, God and the devil, or, more specifically, inner lust and outward Victorian respectability, there are two sides to everything.

When it comes to business, nature's duality takes the form of numbers on a balance sheet. Sometimes, it seems, financial figures just don't add up. While on the surface they may seem to show strong performance, further scrutiny reveals a secret weakness. So make sure to study the balance sheet of a potential investment under a microscope; you never know what these crafty CFOs are trying to *hyde.*

Biz note: *Jekyll and Hyde* can also mean the good and bad qualities of a corporate manager or a volatile stock that fluctuates wildly in price.

Jekyll-and-Hyde Situation

A Jekyll-and-Hyde situation is a predicament in which two officials of a company have important but conflicting goals. Here are some example scenarios:

- Exec 1 wants to use the bulk of last year's income to develop therapeutics to treat polio. Exec 2 reminds him that polio has already been cured. Idiot.
- Exec 2 proposes that the official language of the office be Yiddish. Exec 1 says that Yiddish is a dying language, particularly in Mexico City, where the company is located.
- Exec 2 believes that the company should accept a generous offer to be bought out by a larger, rival company. Exec 1 reminds her partner that she inherited this company from her parents and will never sell it. She threatens to kill Exec 2 if he ever mentions it again.
- Exec 1 believes that the company could be the largest retail clothing chain on the West Coast. Exec 2 reminds his partner that they're located in Newark.
- Exec 1 believes that company employees should be allowed four weeks vacation. "What is this, Switzerland?" remarks Exec 2. "Give them a week unpaid during Christmas and that's it. This is America, for Christ's sake!"
- Exec 1 wants to buy ten more delivery vehicles. Exec 2 thinks it's unnecessary. They compromise on five rickshaws.
- Exec 1 wants to finance expansion with debt, while Exec 2 wants to give away equity. They decide to just buy lottery tickets.

- Exec 1 wants to focus on developing drugs to fight cancer. Exec 2 reminds Exec 1 that they're in the used-car business.
- Exec 1 wants to have a Chanukah sale and Exec 2 wants to have a Christmas sale. They settle on a Kwanzaa sale, noting that Jesus was a Jew and quite possibly black.

Getting Along

Recently, when Exec 1 proposed that the company invest in bulking up its sales force more than 50 percent over the next year, Exec 2 surprisingly agreed. They hired another salesperson.

JET BLUED

Bringing Humanity Back to Air Travel

WHAT IT MEANS:
To spend more time on the runway than in flight

Founded in February 1999 under the name NewAir, Jet Blue's executives include several former Southwest Airlines employees. JetBlue started by following Southwest's approach of offering low-cost travel but sought to distinguish itself by its amenities, such as in-flight entertainment. In CEO David Neeleman's own words, JetBlue looks "to bring humanity back to air travel."

Blue Balled

In the midst of a snowstorm at New York City's John F. Kennedy International Airport in February 2007, a JetBlue flight headed for Cancun, Mexico, was stranded on the tarmac for nearly nine hours. Passengers were kept inside the plane the entire time. On that same cold February day, at least nine other JetBlue planes were stranded on the tarmac for over eight hours.

A typical flight from New York City to Cancun takes around four hours. So when these passengers got out of the plane, if nothing had gone wrong, they would already have landed in Mexico, made it to town, checked into the hotel, and be at the beach drinking a piña colada. Talk about the blues.

JETTIQUETTE

Ready, Set, Jet . . . iquette!

WHAT IT MEANS:
The rules that govern polite behavior on an airplane

With all the traveling that's required for conducting business and all the hassles involved in flying, it's probably time to consider becoming an OPEN-COLLAR WORKER. Until then, however, you're stuck in the sky with less space, less food, and more rules.

To Air Is Human

A portmanteau of *jet* and *etiquette, jettiquette* is becoming more complicated every day. Not only are there always new rules involving things like lighters, Chapstick, cell phones, and shoes, but now you must partially disrobe to get on the plane. "Nothing like getting naked with strangers," I say to women as I take off my shoes, my jacket, and my belt. I've had moderate successes with this line. (Go ahead, use it.)

Though everyone is frightened of terrorists, malfunctions, and midair collisions today, as the hours pass, people begin to stop worrying and start complaining as their bottoms become numb, their legs begin to ache, and the stomachs start to growl.

But this doesn't make complaining okay. You still have to be polite. Here's a little refresher on contemporary jettiquette:

THINGS TO AVOID WHILE FLYING

- Joining the mile-high club
- Sleeping on your neighbor's shoulder
- Having seven Bloody Marys (It's a plane, not a bar)
- Talking about famous plane wrecks

THINGS TO DO

- Ambien
- Another Grisham novel
- Watch *24* on your iPod
- Listen to your boring neighbor talk about his cats

✚ **FIRST COINED**: Alan Peppard, "Chucking the Social Life," *Dallas Morning News,* October 1995.

JOB-LOSS RECOVERY

Win Some, Lose Some

WHAT IT MEANS:

A recovery in the economy that is accompanied by an overall loss in the total number of jobs

The years after the turn of the century proved difficult for the American economy. But it had nothing to do with Y2K. No, after the dot-com bubble burst, the next few years brought an economic recovery. However, the beginning of this recovery saw a decrease in the number of jobs. Hence, the term *job-loss recovery.* The term is a play on the phrase *jobless recovery* (economic growth that doesn't create new jobs), which dates back to the economic woes of the early eighties.

Economists still can't agree about the causes and cures of job-loss and jobless recoveries. Some argue that increased productivity through automation and robotics has allowed economic growth without creating new jobs. Other economists suggest that they stem from structural change in the labor market, leading to unemployment as workers change jobs or industries.

Some have suggested that free trade is a possible cause. In this view, during lean times companies are more likely to move factories and jobs offshore to cut costs. These jobs generally don't come back after the economy improves.

➕ **FIRST COINED**: Kenneth N. Gilpin, "U.S. Economy Grew Slowly in First Period," *International Herald Tribune,* April 2003.

JOB SPILL

It Never Ends

Job spill is nearly taken for granted by employers these days. Just because some putz stayed late all

WHAT IT MEANS:
Work or work-related tasks that carry over into personal time

the time before, now you're expected to do the same. Don't do it unless you get some equity.

You remember Bill Lumbergh in *Office Space:* "Yeeeeaaahh, I'm also gonna need you to go ahead and come in on Sunday, too . . . yeeeaaahhh."

HOW TO AVOID JOB SPILL
- Say "no" to overtime. Seriously, try it.
- Keep busy during the day. If you're on top of your work, you'll avoid a lot of job spill that you may cause yourself.
- Don't tell your boss anything about your personal life. When he asks you to do something unreasonable, say you can't. Don't explain. If he asks, say, "It's personal."
- Turn off your cell phone when you get home. Whatever it is can wait until tomorrow.
- Don't get too snuggly with your coworkers. They'll rat you out in a second if there's something in it for them.

Work As a Religion

We're up against a lot. Your boss wants you to be a believer in her company, even though you have only a tiny stake in the matter. She wants you to be a good little lamb: a follower of her ten commandments.

The Ten Work Commandments

I. Thou shalt have no other life outside work.

II. Thou shalt not download any craven images.

III. Thou shalt not take the name of thy boss in vain.

IV. Remember the Sabbath day to work and keep it holy.

V. Honor thy office and its policies.

VI. Thou shalt not kill time.

VII. Thou shalt not commit adultery with interns.

VIII. Thou shalt not steal thy boss's Post-it notes.

IX. Thou shalt not wantonly photocopy thy backside.

X. Thou shalt not covet thy neighbor's cubicle.

✚ **FIRST COINED**: Jill Andresky Fraser, *White-Collar Sweatshop: The Deterioration of Work and Its Rewards in Corporate America,* W. W. Norton & Company, February 2001.

KIPPER

Kids: Are They Really Worth It?

WHAT IT MEANS:
An adult who still lives at home with his or her parents

Kippers, an acronym for "kids in parent's pockets eroding retirement savings," are not few and far between. They're right down the block. In fact, many of your friends may fit this definition. (Relax, I didn't say *you*.)

Despite common belief, kippers are not necessarily unmotivated, and many have full-time jobs. Perhaps they just recognize a good thing and are holding on with all their might, knowing that mommy would never kick her favorite baby out, no matter how much he ate or how many times he came home after curfew.

Kipper International

While American parents might spend their days at work plotting arranged marriages to get rid of their kipper, in most countries this is the norm. Take Italian men, who usually live at home well into their thirties. In fact, the Italian *mommoni* gave us our English term "mama's boy."

K

HOW TO KNOW IF YOU'RE DATING A KIPPER

- He always wants to hook up at your place.
- He tells you that the reason he can afford to buy rounds at the bar is because his "roommates" pay most of the rent.
- On his behalf, his mom proposed to you.
- All of his clothes are perfectly ironed.
- He has thumb twitch from playing too many video games.

✚ **FIRST COINED:** In a 2003 survey from Prudential.

KITCHEN SINK

Bombs Away

{ **WHAT IT MEANS:**
To announce all of a company's bad financial news at one time

Dating back to World War II, the old phrase "Everything but the kitchen sink" originally referred to heavy bombing in which it seemed like the enemy was firing well, everything but the kitchen sink.

Nowadays in business, the saying refers to the gruesome event when a company decides to announce all of its financial failures at once. But while the explosion is deadly for shareholders, the idea is that it would be even more deadly to announce each bit of bad news individually. Think of it as tearing off a bandage quickly rather than a little at a time.

➕ **FIRST COINED:** This sense of the phrase was first printed in Martin Winn's article, "Ferranti Set to Unveil Big Losses," *The Independent,* July 1990.

LAKE WOBEGON EFFECT

Mama's Boy

WHAT IT MEANS:
The tendency to overestimate one's achievements and potential

It started with your mom: "You're the most attractive and brightest person in the world," she might have said as she tucked you in. Of course, you weren't. And then came your second-grade teacher: "You're all special, each and every one of you," she might have said to the class. Of course, that too was crap, unless by "special" she meant that each kid had a unique set of fingerprints or a distinctive amount of freckles—and then yes, you were all special indeed. But that's not what she meant. She meant, like many teachers do, that each kid was above average or exceptional in some way. But unfortunately, that just ain't true. After all, by definition, half the children are above the national average and half are below it. Thank goodness for that statistics teacher in college—even if he was sort of a jerk.

To Sink or Swim

While confidence is crucial in corporate America, the Lake Wobegon effect can create unrealistic expectations for both individuals and companies. This desire may even lead a company board to raise a CEO's paycheck when she doesn't deserve it, just because they want to give the impression that they've got the biggest big shot in town.

The term *Lake Wobegon effect* is derived from the fictional town of Lake Wobegon, Minnesota, from humorist Garrison Keillor's 1985 novel, *Lake Wobegon Days,* where, "all the women are strong, all the men are good-looking, and all the children are above average."

Hmm, so that's why people actually live in Minnesota.

Are You Treading Water in Lake Wobegon?

Take this test to determine whether or not you too suffer from an inflated view of yourself. Answer the following questions true or false:

- You believe that, despite the fact that the new guy is young, has a Harvard MBA, and moonlights as a concert pianist and underwear model, you're still a better catch than he is.
- You believe that you could do more cocaine than Robert Downey Jr. and survive to tell the tale.
- You could have easily been an astronaut; you just prefer marketing.
- Being a famous comedian would be easy for you. Remember Gallagher?
- You could be a supermodel. It's all airbrushing anyway.
- Bill Gates just got lucky. You would have done just as well if you knew about that computer stuff at the time.
- You're just as smart as those people at NASA. They're just good at science.
- You should be promoted to CEO. So what if you don't have an MBA? Business school is just nonsense anway. You've got street smarts.

If you answered more than two in the affirmative, we suggest you seek help before you drown in your own delusions.

⊕ **FIRST COINED:** Christopher Connell, "Education Official Says Achievement Tests Paint Unrealistic Picture," Associated Press, February 1988.

LATTE FACTOR

StarBUCKS . . . You Got That Right

--{ **WHAT IT MEANS:**
Spending a little bit of money here and there adds up in the long run

"I'll have a grande, nonfat, cinnamon, hazelnut latte with whipped cream, strawberries, and a twist of lemon. Oh, could you crumble up some chocolate cookies and three blue-cheese olives in there, too?"

As coffee gets more complex, it also gets more expensive. And, believe it or not, little daily purchases like soda, coffee, cigarettes, and other junk can start to add up. Cut these expenses out of your budget and put it aside, and you might be sitting on a million dollars one day.

Five Bucks a Day

All you have to do is set aside a few bucks a day and you could wind up richer than your wildest dreams—even if you're currently living paycheck to paycheck.

Still not convinced?

$5 per day × 7 days = $35 per week

$35 per week = $150 per month

$150 per month invested at a rate of 10 percent annual return =

1 year = $1,885	15 years = $62,171
2 years = $3,967	30 years = $339,073
5 years =$11,616	40 years = $948,611
10 years = $30,727	

Now, that sure beats a caffeine rush!

⊕ **FIRST COINED:** Investment guru and bestselling author David Bach.

LAYOFF LUST

Fire Away!

WHAT IT MEANS:
The desire to be fired from one's job

For the majority of their careers, American employees live in fear of their boss. "I hope I don't get fired," says the frightened, down-trodden worker every time his or her superior is in an uproar. But despite this life of quiet desperation, sometimes getting fired is the best thing that can happen to you.

With unemployment benefits unavailable to employees who quit, getting canned is the only way that most employees can afford to move on. And so what if you can't use your former employer as a reference? Chances are that no one will ever check anyway.

Best Ways to Get Fired

If you are going to be let go, you might as well provoke your boss in an exciting and memorable way. Here are some of the most fun ways to get fired once and for all:

- Stare at his wife's ass when she visits the office.
- Relieve yourself in the wastepaper basket under your desk.
- Don't do anything.
- Practice your Mandarin Chinese with customers.
- Start eating road kill for lunch.
- Stay home.
- Keep calling in sick, over and over again.
- Sacrifice a goat in the conference room and claim religious freedom as a defense.
- Have sex with your boss' secretary.
- Change your legal name to Jacques Strap.

Also, you can look to movies for inspiration. One way to get fired is called the 'Jerry Maguire,' which involves writing an emotionally stirring memo that ensures your immediate removal. Make sure to take the goldfish and the lonely single mom.

Finally, whatever you do don't upset your boss too much. Remember Fredo in *The Godfather II?* Steer clear of company fishing trips.

➕ **FIRST COINED:** "Gen X Embraces the Recession by Going to Plan B: Layoff Lust—Headline," *New York Observer,* December 2001.

LIPSTICK EFFECT

Revlon Is a Girl's Best Friend

WHAT IT MEANS:
When consumers substitute comforting items such as lipstick for luxury goods during hard economic times

Let's be honest: Women love to buy things to improve their appearance. An entire paycheck might go to a fancy dress, a pair or earnings, or some boots. And forget about a cute little handbag—that's worth a mortgage payment.

However, despite the bad rap men have given them regarding their spending habits, women are a very practical bunch. In fact, statistics show that women, like their male counterparts, tend to buy less luxury items during economic recessions. But that doesn't mean they can't look and feel good. Statistics also show women substitute these fancy goods for some good old-fashioned fire-engine red lipstick. Interestingly, lipstick sales are the only cosmetics items to benefit from this consumer phenomenon.

MORE COSMETIC EFFECTS

- **The Chapstick effect:** Eskimo chicks don't wear a lot of makeup.
- **The toenail polish effect:** Downtime in heavy traffic (it's true).
- **The mascara effect:** It happens every time it rains.

➕ **FIRST COINED:** Emily Nelson, "Rising Lipstick Sales May Mean Pouting Economy," *Wall Street Journal,* November 2001.

LOW-HANGING FRUIT

Step by Step

{ **WHAT IT MEANS:**
The most easily attainable goal

Before a budding company can accomplish big goals such as beating out Wal-Mart, designing a car that runs on water, or getting Steven Spielberg to bankroll a Mel Gibson film, other shorter-term goals need to be established and met. Here are some classic low-hanging fruits that any young company has got to pick, and keep picking to survive:

- Paying the light bill
- Finding a receptionist who can operate a phone and not sound like a total jerk
- Installing Microsoft Word on the company mainframe
- Deciding between a casual Friday and a casual Friday that encourages wearing Hawaiian shirts
- Discovering a clever way to screw employees out of health insurance

➕ **FIRST COINED:** David Kull, "Knowing When to Shout 'Eureka!'," *Computer Decisions,* June 1984.

MARZIPAN LAYER

Have Your Cake and Eat It Too!

WHAT IT MEANS:

The level of executives in a company just below the board members or top officers

From the mailroom to the boardroom, there are many levels and layers in the corporate hierarchy. And, like the layers of cake, the closer you are to the top, the sweeter it gets. But while the icing is certainly the sweetest part, the layer just below, sometimes made of marzipan—a paste made from almonds, sugar, and egg whites—is definitely delicious as well.

Yet, if your sweet tooth is just too ambitious, here are a few suggestions for how you can move up and get a bigger piece of the . . . um, cake.

- On the CEO's birthday, climb out of a cake and give him a very, very thorough and compelling PowerPoint presentation.
- Execute each board member in cold blood (with poisoned marzipan).
- Woo the company's potential partners by sending them cakes on the company's anniversary. Who knows, that might just be the icing on the cake.

➕ **FIRST COINED:** Hamish McRae, "Financial Notebook," *The Guardian,* February 1985.

MASSTIGE

Target Hollywood (There's a Wal-Mart Nearby, Too)

{ WHAT IT MEANS:

A retail category that marries low prices with prestigious and trendy brand names

The difference between movie stars and the average Joe was never as stark as back at the height of Hollywood glamour, during the Great Depression of the 1930s. While the average college-educated American was selling apples in the street, the stars of the silver screen were parading around in the most ostentatious getup they could find at the glitziest venues in town.

Believe it or not, today this is changing. Not only can the average college-educated American (unless he's in manufacturing) find a job other than selling apples, movie stars—while richer than ever—are increasingly found wearing the same clothes, buying the same stuff, and frequenting the same places as you and me.

A portmanteau of *mass* and *prestige,* the masstige phenomenon is blurring the lines between the fabulous and the frugal in ways that are fundamentally changing the retail business world. Retailers like Target, Wal-Mart, and the like, offer such a variety of well-priced, quality products that even the snobby can't resist. The best example of this is IKEA, a company that continues to take Scandinavian minimalism to average living rooms across the globe.

Masstige Moments

As we said, famous celebrities are really no different than you or me. Here are some examples of celebrities caught in a masstige moment:

- Tom Cruise caught wearing sweatpants from Marshall's to a Scientology meeting

- Nicole Richie caught eating a Big Mac—okay, wishful thinking.
- Angelina Jolie caught buying goat's milk in some African shantytown.

➕ **FIRST COINED:** "Marketing Toiletries, Cosmetics & Fragrances Conference on Beauty Product Advertising in Mass Media," *Cosmetics International,* March 1996.

MATADOR

Olé!

Every office has a matador, someone whose true business skill lies in dodging assignments and avoiding responsibility. These sneaky characters will stop at nothing to avoid doing work, leaving you to take up the slack.

Enough Bull

Tired of doing more than your fair share at the office? Here are some signs that a matador might be to blame.

REASONS TO SUSPECT YOUR COLLEAGUE IS A MATADOR

- He reads a lot of Hemingway.
- His name is Jim. But he insists you call him "matador."
- He dresses unusually fancifully for an accountant.
- Everything that comes out of his mouth is bullshit.
- He was caught killing a bull in cold blood during lunch.
- He carries a red cape wherever he goes.
- He says "Olé!" instead of "Excuse me."
- Every year he spends his vacation in Pamplona.

MCI PROJECT

All in the Family

WHAT IT MEANS:

A project financed and built by a network of friends and family

Coined from the "friends and family program" that former telecommunications company MCI was famous for, an MCI project is a business venture started by a close network of friends and family. Though begun by a passionate few, MCI projects can grow into huge companies. In fact, many of the largest corporations today started out as family businesses.

Working with friends and family can have many advantages. You know that you can trust everyone, which breeds company loyalty. But there are some downsides to this closeness as well. Consider the scenario of an incompetent family member who needs to be replaced.

FAMOUS FAMILY BUSINESSES
- The Mafia
- Wal-Mart
- Ford Motor Company (how long they can keep it up remains to be seen)
- *Playboy* magazine (not to mention one of the happiest . . . have you seen Hefner's smile?)
- England (the Windsors)
- The Bush/Exxon/Halliburton administration
- Any authentic ethnic restaurant
- Most liquor stores
- Alabama

➕ **FIRST COINED:** Lisa Lenoir, "A Perfect Pair," *Chicago Sun-Times,* November 2003.

MELT-UP

Melting

WHAT IT MEANS:
The severe overheating of a market that causes prices to rise to unprecedented levels

Just as quickly as a market can fall, a market can rise if hysteria sets in and investors begin buying frantically, at almost any price. Buy at any price? Well, it wasn't so long ago that people were happily paying a hundred dollars per share for overcapitalized, unprofitable Internet stocks.

Melt-ups are worrisome for two reasons: fear of missing out on a great up-swing and fear that the melt-up will be quickly followed by a meltdown.

When people get nutty with their money and melt the market up, it's a sign that they've simply gone nuts and can be easily led, duped, or whipped into a frenzy.

On TheStreet.com, financial writer Jim Griffin lambasted the term for its nonsensical denotation, saying, "Otherwise erudite observers use the phrase 'melt-up' in their analyses. Melt-up? It can't be a well-thought-out market if it is represented by so unlikely an image." In fact, he was right about that, at least in part. This quote comes from 1999.

MIDDLESCENTS

Tune In, Turn On, Drop Out

WHAT IT MEANS:
Professionals between thirty-five and fifty-four who are burned out

Increasingly, and at a younger age, we are becoming discontented and disillusioned with work. In a generation or two, our heirs will all be counting down the days to retirement starting in junior high. According to a report entitled "Managing Middlescence" published by *Harvard Business Review,* "Many mid-career employees are working more, enjoying it less, and looking for alternatives."

112

Do You Have Middlescence?

Here are some telltale signs that you're becoming too worn out, too young.

- On your thirtieth birthday, you treated yourself to a cemetery plot.
- You're deciding between Florida and Arizona for your next home.
- You complain that these new comedians are nothing compared to Johnny Carson.
- You're saving a portion of your weekly allowance for retirement purposes.
- You spend your lunch breaks napping in the lounge.

WAYS TO END THE MIDDLESCENCE PROBLEM

- No fluorescent lighting in the office unless it's a fluorescent light-bulb plant.
- All telephones do not ring, they vibrate like cell phones.
- Cubicles made as, well, cubicles, with six sides to keep out external noise and keep your desk at your preferred temperature.
- Your eighty hours per pay period can be logged at any time over those two weeks.
- Reviews every ninety days, just like the books.

MINI-TENDER OFFER

Little Danger

{ WHAT IT MEANS:

A tender offer for less than 5 percent of a company's stock

Mini-tender offers evade many of the protections that larger tender offers provide, including filing with the SEC.

Most investors welcome tender offers because they provide a rare opportunity to sell securities at a premium above-market price. But you should keep in mind that not all tender offers are equal.

Lowball Mini-Tender Offer

Some bidders make mini-tender offers below market prices, hoping that they'll catch you off guard if you don't compare the offer price to the current price. Others make mini-tender offers at a small premium, betting that the market price will rise before the offer closes. If it doesn't, the scoundrels will extend the offer until it does or simply cancel it.

Here are some steps you should take if you are asked to sell securities through a tender offer:

• Find out whether the offer is a mini-tender offer.
• Get a copy of the offering document.
• Determine whether the bidder has adequate financing.
• Identify the current market price for your securities.
• Find out the final tender offer price after all deductions are taken.
• Ask when you'll be paid for the shares you tender.
• Remember that once you agree to a mini-tender offer, you are probably locked in.

MOON THE GIANT

Man on the Moon

You may have done it from your seat in the school bus or during a frat party in college, but most of us—guys, that is—have probably pulled down our pants and showed our tush to the world at least once.

WHAT IT MEANS: To snub a more powerful competitor

The verb *to moon* is defined as, "To expose the buttocks in public, usually as a prank or show of disrespect." Interestingly, this term entered into the American vernacular, according to the *Random House Historical Dictionary of American Slang,* when a character named Moon in the 1958 film *Beatniks* warns, "One more word . . . and I'm gonna *moon* you."

The Dark Side of the Moon

In the business world, there are higher stakes to mooning than in junior high, especially when a smaller company has the chutzpah to moon a larger rival that could kick their butt—metaphorically, of course.

One of the best examples of this was the squabble between giant Microsoft and new company on the block Crossgain Corp. in 2000. Here's how the mooning went down:

1. **A New Pair of Pants**

   Crossgain, a software development company, is founded by former Microsoft big shots Adam Bosworth and Rod Chavez in February, 2000. Many other Microsoft employees join.

2. **Unbuckling the Belt . . . Slowly**

   Crossgain starts recruiting even more Microsoft employees to the giant's dismay.

3. **Unzipping**

   Crossgain decides to develop their service using products from Microsoft rivals Sun Microsystems and Oracle.

4. **Mooning the Giant**

   Crossgain raises $10 million from venture funds, including one run by Microsoft arch-rival former Netscape Communications CEO James Barksdale.

M

5. The Giant's Response . . .

Microsoft didn't just stand by idly and take in an eye full of tuckus. The company accused twenty-three ex-Microsoft employees at Crossgain of violating their noncompete agreements. Microsoft President Steven A. Ballmer rejects appeals to squash the beef.

6. A Compromise?

Microsoft offers to ignore the noncompete issue if Crossgain commits to building its service with Microsoft software.

7. A Full Moon

After testing Microsoft software, Crossgain decides not to use it. The company dismisses the twenty-three ex-Microsoft employees to tiptoe around the noncompete issue, with plans to rehire those workers when their one-year noncompete periods end.

8. Aftermath

Crossgain survives the moon, and thrives. The company was acquired by BEA Systems, Inc., in July, 2001.

M

MOON ROCKET

IPO Liftoff! Sorry, You Missed It . . .

WHAT IT MEANS:

A company with a stock price that rises dramatically following an IPO

Despite efforts to change Wall Street's practices, big investment banks still make sure their best clients get access to IPO shares, leaving out people like you and me. Those privileged enough to get in early on the right deals can make out like a bandit. In 2004, Shopping.com went public. The deal was priced by investment bankers at $18 per share, meaning investors with connections to the right Wall Street bankers could pick up the stock at that price—lucky bastards. The stock opened at $23 and finished its first day near $29, giving those insiders a hefty gain. The IPO game is rigged, but you can still latch on, just like a STAG, and chew the scraps the investment bankers throw from the table.

For the first quarter of 2007, here's how the best and worst IPOs performed. If you look at this chart, you'll see that latching on early and dumping them at the end of the day would have made you great returns.

BIGGEST WINNERS

Company Name	Offer Price	Close Price (First Day)	Percent Change
Fortress Investment Group LLC	$18.50	$31.00	68%
Accuray Incorporated	$18.00	$28.47	58%
AeroVironment, Inc.	$17.00	$23.93	41%
BigBand Networks, Inc.	$13.00	$17.00	31%
FCStone Group, Inc.	$24.00	$31.13	30%
Aruba Networks, Inc.	$11.00	$14.15	29%
Capital Product Partners L.P.	$21.50	$26.75	24%
National CineMedia, Inc.	$21.00	$25.67	22%
Optimer Pharmaceuticals, Inc.	$7.00	$8.50	21%

BIGGEST LOSERS

Company Name	Offer Price	Close Price (First Day)	Percent Change
Xinhua Finance Media Limited	$13.00	$11.35	−13%
Synta Pharmaceuticals Corp.	$10.00	$9.09	−9%
3SBio Inc.	$16.00	$14.85	−7%
GSI Technology, Inc.	$5.50	$5.29	−4%
Oculus Innovative Sciences, Inc.	$8.00	$7.80	−3%
Tongjitang Chinese Medicines	$10.00	$9.75	−3%
Cellcom Israel Ltd.	$20.00	$19.54	−2%
Clearwire Corporation	$25.00	$24.62	−2%
Flagstone Reinsurance Holdings	$13.50	$13.48	0%

M

As you can see, the number-ten spot in the negative side closed at the opening price. Also, the winners were bigger winners than the losers were losers. This doesn't hold true for every quarter. To find out more statistical information about IPOs, check out Hoovers.com IPO central.

MUCUS TROOPER

Stay Home, Please!

WHAT IT MEANS:
An employee with a cold or the flu who insists on showing up for work

While bosses don't like it when you miss work, they don't exactly like it when you show up with a radish for a face and snot dribbling out of your nose. No one likes to sit next to someone who is sick, especially in the United States, where we aren't exactly sensitive to the infirm.

"Oh, you're sick. Would you mind quarantining yourself in a small room?" That's what we say in this country when even our loved ones aren't feeling well. Sure, we'll go to the deli and bring back chicken noodle soup, but that's about it. For fear of catching it ourselves, we often leave our sick alone in a room to suffer in private. At least, that's how a foreign exchange student of mine during high school described our cultural viewpoint on this matter. Hmm, come to think of it, did we ever let him out of the closet?

And, in the office it's no different. Many of us have steered clear of an infected colleague for fear of getting sick ourselves. Sure, it's admirable that this mucus trooper will trek all the way to the office to work under such physical distress, but let's just name him employee of the month and send him home. But with only five sick days a year and a week's vacation, is it any wonder why there are so many poor mucus troopers battling it out in corporate America?

Go Home Trooper!

Managers have a responsibility to keep the workplace productive while also looking out for employee well-being. Tell your mucus trooper to go home even if he insists on showing up to work like so:

- Covered in third-degree burns
- Carrying his right arm in his left
- Holding a dead chicken while passing out surgical masks to coworkers
- Wrapped in a body cast
- Bleeding profusely from the eyes
- With a priest
- On a stretcher
- Hooked up to an IV
- Major head trauma
- In an ambulance
- Wearing a hospital wristband
- With two nurses and a doctor
- With an insurance agent handing out release forms
- Asking people what their blood type is
- Offering money for any information about a spare kidney

➕ **FIRST COINED:** "Up Front: Vital Statistics," *The Observer,* November 2003.

MULTISLACKING

Alt Tab

In case you don't know, I'm going to teach you how to quickly swap between windows. Pressing Alt Tab will shuffle through the open win-

{ **WHAT IT MEANS:**

Having two browser windows open—a personal site and a work-related one—so that you can quickly click to the legitimate site when a manager is nearby

dows on your computer, allowing you to hide porn, MySpace, and Craigslist, and reveal what you should be working on when your boss comes by to harass you about some triviality. Now, in Windows Vista, there are little "Show Desktop" and "Switch between windows" buttons near where the start menu button used to be (now a little Windows flag is there).

Why Multislack?

Because there comes a point in most jobs where there is absolutely no incentive to work faster, better, or smarter. You could send that report to your boss a few days before it's needed, but then you would get another assignment. And who wants that? What to do? Multislack. Or, maybe try a little SUNLIGHTING, if you can get the work.

NAGFLATION

Disaster Will Strike

Another portmanteau, *nagflation* is a combination of *nag* and *inflation*. Market and economic naysayers come on television weekly

WHAT IT MEANS:
The fire-and-brimstone market prognostications from analysts constantly warning us that disaster is about to strike

saying that there are imminent economic dangers. About every decade or so, these pessimists get it right. And, feeling justified, they spend a year doing their segment as an "I told you so" before they get back to warning of another Vesuvian explosion on the horizon.

Famous Pessimists

Woody Allen
Marvin the Paranoid Android
Arthur Schopenhauer
Eeyore

Z

Thomas Malthus
Jean-Paul Sartre
Sigmund Freud
Friedrich Nietzsche
Martin Heidegger
Frederick Douglass
W. E. B. DuBois
Judas Iscariot
Marcus Junius Brutus
Tsar Nicholas II
H. P. Lovecraft

"Do you know what a pessimist is? A man who thinks everybody is as nasty as himself, and hates them for it."

George Bernard Shaw

"The optimist proclaims that we live in the best of all possible worlds; and the pessimist fears this is true."

James Branch Cabell

"Many an optimist has become rich by buying out a pessimist."

Robert G. Allen

Z

NANNY BUBBLE

I Want My Nanny

Having a nanny is bliss. Make a mess, they clean it up. Get hungry, they cook something for you. Feel frisky, they . . . well, it depends on your terms of reference.

{ **WHAT IT MEANS:**

The rising cost of hiring a nanny during a strong economy or stock-market bubble

But nannies aren't cheap, especially in nanny bubbles, when everyone seems to be able to afford one (except, of course, for the nannies themselves). During these good economic times, when the stock market is bursting and jobs are plentiful, nannies can charge anywhere from $30,000 to $40,000 per year. Add to that perks like food, gym memberships, complimentary cell phones, and even trips overseas, and nanny costs can start to hurt—particularly when the bubble suddenly bursts.

Do You Need a Nanny?

Here are some signs that you should bear the costs and hire the help:

- Your children are really, really starting to get on your nerves.
- Your sex life just isn't what it used to be.
- You only have a butler, and that's just not enough help.
- You want a reason to come home.

The perfect nanny . . .

- Stands at about five-foot-ten
- Exercises religiously
- Speaks with a Parisian accent
- Thinks that the only thing more exciting than cleaning is cooking
- Considers clothing to be "too constricting."

➕ **FIRST COINED:** "'Nanny Bubble' Devastates Wall Street," *Corriere della Sera,* July 1998.

NAP NOOK

Working 9 to Zzzz

WHAT IT MEANS:

An office or room where employees can nap during work hours

In America, we've got it all wrong. Sure, we know how to be productive, but sometimes overwork can stress us out to the point that it can actually hurt production.

To recharge our batteries, lunch is an important time for employees. But what do we get in the States? An hour if you're lucky, most of which you spend in line with all the other worker bees. By the time you blow another $10 on a meatball sub, it's time to hurry back to your desk so you can shove it down before it's time to go back to work. Now, with your stomach uncomfortably full, you've got to go over that PowerPoint and prepare for that important meeting. Yep, lunches in corporate America just plain suck. But it isn't like this everywhere.

Take Spain, home of Cervantes, the flamenco, and bullfighting. This great nation's biggest contribution to world culture, however, is the siesta, a period of the day devoted to eating, drinking, and sleeping. Now, that's the way lunch was meant to be.

Back in the good ol' US of A, some employers are realizing that a little nap during the work day can increase the output of their employees, relieving stress and helping them reboot their brains. These forward-looking employers have gone so far as creating a nap nook, a secluded lounge where worker bees can catch their much needed Zs.

While the nap nook sounds nice, in corporate America, the idea can take on a new life, and you'll never leave your job (think Google).

Z

Other "nooks" employers are considering:

- Yoga nook
- Doctor nook
- Massage nook
- Barber nook
- Breakfast nook
- Gummi Bear nook
- Sex nook
- Laundry nook
- Fencing nook
- Church nook
- Divorce-court nook
- Chapel nook
- Used-car lot nook
- Bank nook
- Hospital nook
- Wal-Mart nook
- Yankee Stadium nook
- Psychiatrist nook

NASCAR EFFECT

NIKETOYOTAIBMHUSTLER-
FRITOLAYCISCOMOUNTAINDEW

Whatever. It's just noise. Noise. At least, that's what it seems like initially. But words, unlike cars and other noisemakers, express ideas. Even when words get seemingly lost in a NASCAR effect, they can trigger something in our brain to recognize them. That little recognition can trigger us to buy a pair of Nikes, drive a Toyota, or make us prefer IBM to other computers.

WHAT IT MEANS:

The result of placing too many advertisements or logos in a small space, such as on racecars

Advertising 101

People constantly say that advertisements don't affect them, that they choose products solely based on quality. While that's sometimes true, it more likely is not. Here are a few products the appeal of which is hard to recognize:

- Wonder Bread: The only thing to wonder about this product is how anyone could possibly eat it.
- Slim Jim: Have you actually tasted one of these?
- *The Blair Witch Project:* Terrible movie that grossed huge dollars based on a smart Net-based ad campaign.

NASDAQ

The Nasdaq Nasdaqed!

WHAT IT MEANS:
To sharply decline in value or quantity

Ever since the bubble burst, Nasdaq hasn't been able to reclaim its former glory. From 1999 to 2000, the Nasdaq composite index jumped 100 percent, from about 2,500 to 5,000. Just over a year later, it bottomed out at just over 1,000. Even today, it's at around half of its all-time high.

Strangest uses of the verb *nasdaq:*

- The LSD supply in San Francisco has really nasdaqed since the feds busted Jimmy Acid.
- Ever since my wife got a new job, our sex life has nasdaqed.
- The amount of gas I use has nasdaqed since I bought a hybrid.
- I've really nasdaqed my drinking since my DUI.

Z

NEARSHORING

There's No Place Like Close to Home

WHAT IT MEANS:

Moving company jobs to a nearby foreign country

Moving business operations overseas is nothing new. Western companies have long been going to places like China and India in order to tap into cheaper labor. But despite the cost savings, doing business clear across the globe has its problems for American and European companies. That's why many of them are now looking closer to home. Germany is looking to Poland, Italy to Serbia, and the United States to Mexico. These nations offer a cheaper place to do business, while also being only a hop, skip, and a jump away.

If this trend persists, pretty soon countries like Vietnam will look to Cambodia, Costa Rica to Panama, Turkmenistan to Uzbekistan, and South Korea to North Korea. Okay, maybe not quite yet.

✚ **FIRST COINED:** "Neoit.com Offers to Manage Outsourcing," *Business Line,* July 2002.

NEGATIVE PATIENT OUTCOME

Negative Outcome Patients Go to Heaven

WHAT IT MEANS:

Doctorspeak for "the patient died"

Dead is such a nasty, four-letter word, especially when there might be a hint of malpractice. That's why leading hospital bureaucrats and malpractice lawyers prefer the more concise, less emotional *negative patient outcome.* There's no better way to say "We didn't screw up" than by using words that no one understands.

Which begs the question: Do obstetricians have "positive patient outcomes"?

126

Sample Usage

Doctor: Mrs. Hanson, we're sorry to tell you that during your husband's hernia operation, my scalpel slipped and we. . . .

Malpractice Lawyer: . . . we experienced a negative patient outcome.

Mrs. Hanson: That's great! When can I see him?

Doctor: You can't, Mrs. Hanson, he passed away.

Malpractice Lawyer: Had a negative outcome.

Doctor: Will you knock it off!

NEGATIVE PROFIT

Doublespeak

WHAT IT MEANS:

A loss

Doublespeak is distinguished from jargon in that doublespeak attempts to confuse and conceal the truth, while jargon often provides greater precision to those who understand it (while potentially confusing those who do not). Perhaps the term *negative profit* is used to confuse people. Perhaps it is used simply for the sake of jargon creation. Either way, a negative profit is bad, and don't let corporate executives and investor relations companies tell you differently.

OTHER EXAMPLES OF CORPORATE DOUBLESPEAK
- RIGHTSIZING for layoffs
- Reliability enhancement for fixing a software bug
- Negative cash flow for losing money
- Biosolids for sewage
- Corporate communications for corporate propaganda

NERDISTAN

Revenge of the Nerds

What do Bill Gates, Steve Jobs, and Larry Ellison have in common? Yes, billions of dollars, but what else?

They're nerds—complete and total nerds. You know, the kind of kids who got bullied between classes and couldn't get a date to the prom. But that was then and this is now. These guys won't ever have to go stag again.

Defined as "persons who are single-minded or accomplished in scientific or technical pursuits but are felt to be socially inept," nerds play an increasingly important role in the Internet-driven economy. Gravitating toward fields like computers and high technology, wherever there's a tech boom there's a nerdistan—you can count on it.

FAMOUS NERDISTANS

Silicon Valley, California
South Orange County, California
Route 128, outside Boston, Massachusetts
Silicon Alley, Manhattan
Redmond, Washington (Microsoft's home base)
North Dallas
South Korea

When in Nerdistan . . .

. . . speak as the nerds do. Here's a list of phrases translated from nerdspeak to common English. Talk about overly technical.

Nerdspeak: Making a long-term substantial familial acquisition
Translation: Buying a dog

Nerdspeak: Forging a strategic merger of equal entities
Translation: Getting married

Nerdspeak: Initiating a biologically imperative fueling process using a combination of various cheeses, sliced ham, and bits of pineapple
Translation: Eating Hawaiian pizza

Nerdspeak: Analyzing operational risks associated with cohabitation of potential familial liabilities
Translation: Worrying about the in-laws moving in

Nerdspeak: An initial rollout of a strategic recreational venture in a Southern California–based entertainment complex
Translation: Taking your kids to Disneyland for the first time

Nerdspeak: Developing a proprietary familial asset
Translation: Having a baby

Nerdspeak: Implementing a central multimedia imaging and sound system for the purpose of creating a long-term entertainment facility which all family partners can utilize
Translation: Buying an entertainment center for your living room

Nerdspeak: Disengaging a strategically unnecessary and potentially hazardous biological by-product
Translation: Going number two

Z

✚ **FIRST COINED:** Joel Kotkin, "Escape from Nerdistan," *Washington Post,* September 1997.

NEW GUY GENE

Putting Your Foot in Your Mouth

{ **WHAT IT MEANS:**

When new employees lay low until they are comfortable with their coworkers and environment

The danger of not keeping quiet is the possibility of offending someone who might rat you out to the boss. If a cat-lover hears your tirade about how worthless cats are, he may be as offended as if you were talking about his kid. And if that can be a touchy subject, don't go near comments about races, creeds, sexual orientation, disabilities, religions and all the other junk in the anti-discrimination law. That's just asking for trouble. And a sure way to create an uncomfortable working environment for yourself is to make everyone hate you. Trust me, I know.

HONING YOUR NEW GUY GENE

- Never comment on your coworker crush until you're sure he's not sleeping his way up (or down) the corporate ladder.
- Don't overwork. People who have been with the company for longer than you will resent you for making them look lazy.
- Don't take the last piece of pizza at the office luncheon—unless no one's looking.
- Remain politically correct until you identify fellow wise-guys. Even then, be sure to converse with them only when you know no one else is around.
- Never gossip with the secretaries. You can't trust them.

Z

NINJA LOAN

Hobo Loan

A NINJA loan requires nothing other than your being alive, and even that may be a soft rule. If you

were homeless, you could walk into a lender's office, tell them you're a millionaire, and be able to get a giant loan for a huge home that you couldn't afford to make one payment on.

New Paradigm?

No way. For about a half decade, all you had to do to make money was keep upgrading your house. As this phenomenon occurred, more and more people started figuring out the game. This included lending businesses. They figured that all they had to do was give a loan to any living person and leave the housing market to make everyone involved loads of cash.

Then it stopped. People forgot that housing could be speculative. Now, people are sitting on junk loans they can't afford to pay with houses so large they can't afford to fill them. American Dream, baby. American Dream.

Mickey Mouse Loans

During the last housing boom, over half of borrowers were able to get loans based on little more than their stated income. Lenders didn't bother to verify the amounts and spread their cash generously around the country.

For speculative players, the loans were a good opportunity. They could buy much more house than their incomes would usually allow, and, if they could flip them quickly, they could reap giant profits. One lender sampled 100 loan applicants and found that ninety had exaggerated take-home pay by 5 percent

Z

or more and that nearly sixty inflated their pay by over 50 percent. Even on a loan that doesn't require the buyer to prove his income, lying on the application is a federal crime.

Some experts believe that America's recent real estate boom was largely fueled by weakened standards that sparked excessive demand and drove up prices. Some have speculated that the lax standards also sparked a huge expansion of fraud.

More egregious fraud also thrived. An "M. Mouse" received one of these loans. D. Duck was denied a loan, and is now filing a discrimination lawsuit against the lender.

Other types of shady loans (hard to believe, but real) that bankers, business, and bimbos thought were a good idea:

- **Balloon mortgage:** The borrower pays only interest for ten years before a big payment is due.
- **Option ARM loan:** The borrower can pay less than what is due, simply by adding to the outstanding balance of the loan.
- **Piggyback loan:** The borrower receives two mortgages, eliminating the need for a down payment.
- **Teaser loan:** This one qualifies the borrower for a loan based on an artificially low initial interest rate, even though he or she don't make enough money to make payments when the interest rate goes up in two years.
- **Stretch loan:** The borrower has to commit more than 50 percent of gross income to make the monthly payments.

NOTE

Not Just Your Average NIMBY

NOTE is the little brother of the good ol' NIMBY ("not in my back yard"). The BANANA ("build absolutely nothing anywhere near anything") and the NOPE ("not on planet Earth") are the little sisters to them both. All of the same ilk, their degrees differ from local, to regional, to global.

WHAT IT MEANS:

An acronym for "not over there, either"; a person or attitude that opposes new real estate development in the local community and is not open to compromise on this issue

NIMBY says: "No power plant in Duluth."

NOTE says: "No power plant in Minnesota."

BANANA and NOPE say: "No power plants in the world!"

Soon to Come

NOISE: Not out in space either

NITU: Nowhere in the universe

EIB: Everything is bad

➕ **FIRST COINED:** David Rowan, "Glossary for the Nineties," *The Guardian,* September 1994.

z

OFFICE CREEPER

To Catch a Thief

{ **WHAT IT MEANS:**
A thief who sneaks into office buildings to steal equipment

Corporate espionage is nothing knew. Business, after all, is war. Since the days of the robber barons, unscrupulous tactics have been used to find out what the competition is up to, and even steal from them to get ahead. However, a new form of thievery has started to spread through corporate America—just good old-fashioned robbery.

Called office creepers, well-dressed burglars are casually entering offices around the country during work hours, particularly during the end of the day when workers are leaving and cleaning crews are arriving. As many employees bring their laptops and other gadgets to work, swiping a nice new MacBook off a desk is like shooting fish in a barrel. The thieves then walk out the front door undetected.

BUSINESSES MOST TARGETED BY OFFICE CREEPERS

- Wall Street brokerage houses (everyone looks like a crook anyway)
- De Beers (with so many diamonds lying around. . . .)
- Software development firms (you think those geeks will put up a fight?)

BUSINESSES OFFICE CREEPERS AVOID

- Any company located in Texas. You don't want to mess around there.
- Companies whose workers are represented by the Teamsters Union
- Companies in Maine (that is Stephen King country after all)

FIRST COINED: Ron Galperin, "Office Buildings Stepping up Security Services," *Los Angeles Times,* June 1990.

OHNOSECOND

Yikes!

In this fast-paced world, small errors can translate into big problems. Accidentally deleting the

{ **WHAT IT MEANS:**
The little bit of time it takes you to realize that you've just made a huge mistake

wrong file, sending an e-mail waywardly, or even the tiniest of misspellings could cost a promotion, a job, or even a career.

Ohnoseconds occur outside the office as well. Turning up a one-way street, calling your husband "Tom" when his name is "Carl" during an intimate moment, and giving your kid the keys to your car are good examples.

BIGGEST "OOPSES"
1. Moments after the captain of the *Exxon Valdez* sobered up
2. Cheney on his infamous hunting trip
3. Howard Dean after finishing his presidential-bid-ending scream

OPEN-COLLAR WORKER

The New American Dream

A long, long time ago, the American Dream was to own a little farm

{ **WHAT IT MEANS:**
A person who works from home

and live off the land. At some point, it turned into putting on a tie and working for a conglomerate. Now, we're getting back to our roots—in spirit, anyway.

O

Working from home allows us to be our own master, focusing our time and energy on what we want. Now, with the Internet, cell phones, e-mail, teleconferencing, and VoIP, there's really no reason to go in some office to conduct our business. We can do it from a cabana on the beachside.

When I Grow up, I Want to Be in Software Sales . . .

Remember all those exciting professions you wanted to try when you were growing up? For you ladies out there, remember how desperately you want to be a famous actress, a veterinarian, or our nation's first woman president? And what about you guys? Remember how badly you wanted to be a firefighter, a police-officer, or a gangster like Al Pacino in *Scarface?* Ah, yes, those were days when the American Dream seemed so close. But after decades of alarm clocks, heavy traffic, day care costs, and office politics, all you really want to be able to do is set up conference calls in your boxer shorts.

Common Open-Collar Worker Professions
Web designers
Writers
eBay moguls
Prostitutes

➕ **FIRST COINED:** "The Small Issue, the Big Picture," *Washington Post,* December 1988.

O

OPEN THE KIMONO

Let's Get It On (If Your Books Are Clean)

Whether or not to go public is a question that many companies

weigh heavily every day. On the one hand, entering the public markets offers the company access to previously inaccessible capital, putting them in touch with a whole new world of investors. On the other hand, being a public company isn't cheap, requiring all sorts of compliance costs that private companies can avoid. Public companies also have to adhere to much stricter rules in terms of disclosure. They also receive a thorough physical examination of their accounting practices, how much they pay their executives, and what the risks are to investors. In short, they've got to let loose and open that kimono.

OVERWORKING CLASS

Overworked or Stressed?

I don't think we can tell the difference. Almost a third of U.S. employees feel overworked by the amount of work they have to do,

according to a study by the Families and Work Institute, a nonprofit organization that conducts research about the changing nature of work and family life.

These people will develop high blood pressure and have heart attacks, or so say modern folklore and television news. But why can't we just have some tea, take a bath, and take a short walk? I suspect that while we know how to work, we don't know how to relax. Try a Xanax.

O

All Work and No Play . . .

. . . makes you boring. But the bills keep stacking up. There are many pipers to pay, and they must be paid. The government, the insurance company, your home lenders—the list goes on and on. How to get a raise? Work more. How to keep your job? Work more. How to earn some extra bucks? Work more.

So, That's All There Is?

Yep, sorry, friend. One day, you'll wake up to find that your kids have moved out, your spouse has left you, and your dog is dead. The good news is that, if you work hard, your bills will be paid and your bank account will be healthy. Congratulations, you're a modern success story!

PERSONAL SHOPPER

Shop Til They Drop

WHAT IT MEANS:
A person hired to shop for you

Between martinis over lunch, sitting on a plane, and attending every Little League game their sons play, many of today's busy business execs just can't find the time to try on the latest line of jeans at Urban Outfitters. For these big shots, a personal shopper is hired to buy everything from designer watches to cereal to electronics.

WHEN TO FIRE YOUR PERSONAL SHOPPER . . .

- You asked for a Blackberry. You got the fruit.
- You asked for a power tie. You got a piano tie.
- You asked for a time piece. You got a grandfather clock.
- You asked for four suits. You got playing cards.
- You asked for beluga. You got bologna.
- You asked for Ginsu knives. You got ginseng and plastic forks.

P

- You asked for him to plan a trip to San Francisco. You got LSD from San Francisco.
- You asked for a briefcase. She put your lawyer on a short retainer.
- You asked for a new gym to work out at. You got a tank-top-clad, muscular man named Jim at your door.

PESTER POWER

Pretty Please with Sugar . . .

WHAT IT MEANS:
The knack children have for nagging their parents into buying things they wouldn't otherwise buy or do things they wouldn't otherwise do

Children can dictate our purchases because they know how to press our buttons. Throwing tantrums in the aisle, giving us that, "I'm so cute" face, and making sure they tell us about all their other friend's parents and how wonderful and generous they are by comparison. But while this sort of power is to be expected, one dangerous question looms: What if these little people had the power to persuade us to do other things? What kind of world would it be?

THE CHILD OF THE FUTURE WILL MAKE US . . .

- Vote for the Nickelodeon party
- Make our bedtime two hours before theirs
- Take nine-month summer vacations
- Install a skateboard lane on the freeway
- Make Disneyland the nation's capital
- Change "breakfast" to "Pop-Tart-fast"
- Change NC-17 to NC-17 months
- Award a Muppet movie "Best Picture of the Year"
- Cut back to two subjects in school: food fighting and video games
- Make us take out the trash and do the dishes

PGST

It's Always Summer Somewhere

The world is not flat. It's spherical. Don't let anyone tell you differently, not even Tom Freidman. Transportation times and capitalist opportunism have made it possible to get an avocado from California

WHAT IT MEANS:

An acronym for "permanent global summertime," the ability to purchase fruits and vegetables from different parts of the world at different times of the year, enabling people to buy produce year round

or Mexico or Chile to New Jersey in time for lunch 365.25 days per year. Sometimes the avocado is great, and sometimes it tastes a little gamey. But better a gamey avocado than no avocado at all. Ask your nutritionist; it's true.

That's a Tomato?

You've bought those beautiful grocery store fruit and veggies before. You were mesmerized by them. They were cosmetically perfect, irresistibly firm, and brilliantly colored. However, when you got them home, they tasted like nothing. You've been conned by your grocer, his deliverer, and permanent global summertime. After all, how else do you expect to get a tomato in the dead of winter in Nova Scotia?

● FIRST COINED: Joanna Blythman, "Strange Fruit," *The Guardian,* September 2002.

P

POPULUXE

Luxury for All

--{ WHAT IT MEANS:

Target, H&M, IKEA, Wal-Mart, etc. These are the stores where Ameri-

Consumer goods that are stylish and cheap

cans drop $20 on a pair of jeans, and walk out feeling like a million bucks. Populuxe. These stores didn't invent these jeans, the $10 shower curtain, or the $100 couch. They made them cool. Sure, it's not quite Gucci cool, but it's cool nonetheless—especially outside Beverly Hills or Fifth Avenue.

The Consumer Revolution

While the consumer revolution has been going strong for decades, only recently has nearly everyone become middle class. If you make between $30,000 and $150,000 per year, consumerism has you all in the same boat. Sure, some of us own our own home; some of us rent. Some of us have health insurance; some of us hope for the best. Some of us drive Corollas; some of us drive Camrys. But we all still go to Wal-Mart and IKEA. Lucky us.

Nostalgia for the 1950s

The word *populuxe* was originally used to describe the futuristic design style of the late 1950s and early 1960s. The populuxe of the time often used pastel colors, synthetic materials, and stainless steel to make people think that they were in luxurious surroundings. While it wasn't all that luxurious, compared to the plastic junk we have around today it seems positively ostentatious.

✚ **FIRST COINED:** Thomas Hines, *Populuxe,* Alfred A. Knopf, October 1986.

POST-AND-PRAY

Lightning Strikes

Your chances of finding a decent job using this method are next to nil. Managers looking to fill a posi-

WHAT IT MEANS:

Posting a resume online and praying that someone responds

tion will likely get overloaded with resumes, and they might even miss good applicants just because of the volume. Unless you harass hiring managers with telephone calls, e-mails, and letters, the strategy you're using is probably more like "send and pray" than applying.

The Power of Prayer

Sometimes those who post-and-pray are lazy. Sometimes they are just too busy and have another job to go through the long and arduous task of applying for new work. While someone without a job might write little essays and fill in all the answers on a test, someone who has a job and is looking for something a little more interesting or something that pays a little better isn't going to bother.

Post and Collect

There is another benefit to posting your resume on a job board. By posting your resume on these Web sites, many government agencies consider you actively searching for a job. Thus, you can still collect unemployment if you've been laid off and want to take a few months to play solitaire.

⊕ FIRST COINED: Karen Robinson-Jacobs, "Functions of Job-Search Dot-Coms Evolving," *Los Angeles Times,* August 2000.

PRAIRIE-DOGGING

Office Rubber-Neckers

- - {**WHAT IT MEANS**:

The sudden appearance of people's heads over the top of the cubicle walls when something interesting or noisy happens

Just like the rubber-neckers on the road that slow you down to get a glimpse of an accident, office rubber-neckers, or prairie-doggers, slow down business. The boss yells at an employee, two minutes of everyone's day is wasted. A coworker gets fired, that's at least ten minutes gone forever. Someone should invent a cubical that has six sides.

Just like on the freeway, people take a look at office mishaps because they want something to talk about, they don't want to miss anything, and office life can be quite a bore. So when the coffeemaker explodes or the boss finally has that heart attack everyone knew was coming, keep an eye on the cubicles, not the mishap.

Most Exciting Prairie-Dogging Moments

Sticking your head where it doesn't belong can sometimes offer you one heck of a view. Here are some of the best office shenanigans to catch a glimpse of:

1. Cubicle sex (obviously)
2. Self-flagellation by a devout coworker
3. Your nemesis being scolded by management

PRESENTEEISM

Whatever Happened to Good Ol' Absenteeism?

WHAT IT MEANS:
Showing up for work despite being too sick, stressed, or distracted to be productive

Gone are the days of skipping a day from work just because it's sunny or you stayed up a little too late. Now, the trend is to go to work even if you're infected with the bubonic plague. In eight hours, you will do thirty minutes of work, expose five of your colleagues to the disease, and cut your life short by about three days. All in a day's work.

Afraid of Your Boss?

Don't be. Make him afraid of you. Here's how:

- Don't ask him if you can do something. Tell him, and then tell him why it's best.
- Mention your mob connections over lunch.
- Join the NRA and have your mail sent to the office.
- Put a picture of you wearing a karate gi and black belt on your desk.
- Have a friend call you at work posing as your sisiter who works for Slip and Fall and Associates law firm.
- Become a fundamentalist Muslim.
- Invite him on a bear-hunting trip. If he accepts, ask him what kind of baseball bat he'll be using.

✚ **FIRST COINED:** Lisa O'Kelly, "Lonely Life on the British Treadmill," *The Observer,* July 1994.

PROCRASTURBATION

Where Has the Day Gone?

{ **WHAT IT MEANS:**
Procrastinating by masturbating

Yet another portmanteau, *procrasturbation* is actually one of the better ways to procrastinate. It certainly beats solitaire.

Best Masturbation Quotes

Everyone has something to say about masturbation. Here are some of our favorite quotes on the subject:

"Don't knock masturbation, it's sex with someone I love."
Woody Allen

"Masturbation: Shaking hands with the unemployed."
George Carlin

"Give a man free hands, and you'll know where to find them."

Mae West

"In the nineteenth century, masturbation was a disease. In the twentieth, it's a cure."

Thomas S. Szasz

"Philosophy is to the real world as masturbation is to sex."
Karl Marx

"The good thing about masturbation is that you don't have to dress up for it."

Truman Capote

"Intercourse with a woman is sometimes a satisfactory substitute for masturbation. But it takes a whole lot of imagination to make it work."

Karl Kraus

P

PROLETARIAN DRIFT

Here Come the Proles

Proletariat is a term used to identify a lower social class. (A member of that a class is a proletarian.) Originally it was identified as those people who had no wealth other than their sons, and was thus often derogatory. Later, Karl Marx used it as a term to refer to the working class.

WHAT IT MEANS:
A tendency for upscale products to eventually become popular with the working class

Poor Joe

Marketers look down on the people they are marketing to (see ROACH BAIT), television programmers sneer at their audiences, salespeople hate their buyers. They think that these people represent the lowest common denominator of society. And they feel that they are either doing the average Joe a public service, or they feel like the world has shafted them by forcing them to deal with good-old Joe.

Writers, on the other hand, think our readers have impeccable taste, are extraordinarily intelligent, and are dashing and attractive.

⊕ FIRST COINED: Curt Suplee, "A Class Critic Takes Aim at America," *Washington Post,* September 1982.

PROSUMER

Proloney

A portmanteau of *professional* and *consumer,* prosumers think that the key to becoming Tiger Woods or Annie Leibovitz is to use the

WHAT IT MEANS:
An amateur who believes he or she has the knowledge and expertise that requires the purchase of professional-level equipment

best driver or camera. Sure, training, practice, and all that jazz are part of it, they think, but a $25,000 camera is all you really need to go pro. Of course, you give a kangaroo a graphite golf club and it's not going to be getting into the Masters.

Business Sense

For years, advertisers have been telling you that if you want to be like Mike, you'll drink Coke and wear Nikes. They don't tell you that you'll also have to be six-foot-six, and be able to lose a million bucks in Vegas on a whim. So, you've got your Nikes and your Coke. You've got a pro basketball. You've even got a Bulls jersey with the number 23 on it. But you're not like Mike. You can't jump. You can't shoot. And you look like a clown.

PROTIREMENT

Work or Life?

The idea of protirement is inspiring. Corporate life is often the dregs. According to one study,

WHAT IT MEANS:
Leaving a career you don't like to pursue work or hobbies that you enjoy

over 80 percent of thirty- to thirty-five-year-olds claim they are unhappy at work. Long working hours and increased pressures have young professionals wondering whether it is worth it.

Many people see a choice in front of them between continuing in a career that pays well but makes them unhappy and doing something that pays less but is more fulfilling. Research suggests that one in fifteen people under thirty-five is already protired.

Worst Protirement Projects

While everyone has different interests, some are just stupid. Here are some of the dumbest exercises on the planet:

- **Acting:** Have you ever been in a play? Either way, don't do it.
- **Writing:** I don't need any more competition.
- **Mining:** Unless you're Canadian, forget about it.
- **Day trading:** Your adversaries are sharks. Have fun in the pool with them.

➕ **FIRST COINED**: Frederic M. Hudson, "The Adult Years: Mastering the Art of Self-Renewal," Jossey-Bass Inc., November 1991.

PUMP AND DUMP

We Just Want to Pump . . . You Up

Traditionally, this illegal scheme was done by cold-calling individual investors, but along with the Internet came the e-mail pump,

> **WHAT IT MEANS:**
> When a shareholder encourages investors to buy a stock in an effort to raise its share price, and then sells his or her shares at the higher price

and the pump-and-dump routine has become even more prevalent. About 15 percent of all spam is pump-and-dump solicitation. A distinguishing factor of pump-and-dump e-mail from nearly all other types of spam is that the senders don't need for you to contact them. Because of this, pump-and-dump spam is harder to fight.

The Company

The pump-and-dump scheme typically starts with a thinly traded micro-cap company that has very few assets. The company's shares usually trade for less than a buck, are easy to manipulate, and are likely listed on the pink sheets because the company doesn't meet the minimum requirements for a listing on a stock exchange (such as the NYSE or NASDAQ). In the preponderance of pump-and-dump schemes, the companies themselves are not behind the scams.

The Pump

After buying shares in the stock, the fraudster sends out spam that promotes the company. The spam might mention upcoming business deals, citing company press releases, along with information from analysts. The messages urge you to get in as soon as possible so you can get a piece of the action.

The Dump

A small portion of the people who receive the e-mail will buy the stock. Even though it's only a few shares, the new interest in the company pushes up the price. The fraudster then sells his shares, taking a profit. The flurry of selling forces the share price right back down again.

CATCH PHRASES FOR PUMP-AND-DUMP PITCHES

- A once-in-a-lifetime opportunity
- Based on insider information
- Has already gone up X percent, and will continue to rise
- Don't miss your chance
- Buy early
- Strong play
- Watch this one take off

PUT SKIN IN THE GAME

Executive Dilemma

The term, coined by investment legend Warren Buffett, refers to when

WHAT IT MEANS: To make a significant investment in a company

insiders use their own money to buy stock in their own company. This helps ensure that the corporation is managed by people who share a stake in the company. After all, the best vote of confidence an executive can make is putting her own money on the line.

Worth Risking Your Neck Over?

Unless you're dealing with other people's money, it's probably not a good idea to overexpose yourself to any one company or product. The more broad your investments, the less risk you take. Unless you own it, no company should occupy more than 5 percent of your portfolio because you don't control the variables that contribute to the company's outcome. You don't have anything to do with product quality, the competitive situation, the price, the sales, customer service, the economic climate, the location, or even the weather.

Now, if 6 or 7 percent of your portfolio is enough for you to become a majority shareholder in a company, it's a different story. If you want that set of headaches (and possible rewards), go for it.

OTHER QUOTABLE BUFFETTISMS

"It takes twenty years to build a reputation and five minutes to ruin it. If you think about that, you'll do things differently."

"Risk comes from not knowing what you're doing."

"Wide diversification is only required when investors do not understand what they are doing."

"If a business does well, the stock eventually follows."

"Only buy something that you'd be perfectly happy to hold if the market shut down for ten years."

PUT SOME PANTS ON IT

The Naked Truth

WHAT IT MEANS:

To fill in the missing details for an idea or concept

Your whole life, you've heard that all it takes is one good idea to make it big. "Remember the guy who came up with the pet rock," your father might have said. "Or the guy who invented sticky notes. All it takes is one idea like that, and you're rich."

While that may be true, it takes more than just a vague concept to bring home the bacon. For ideas to be translated into products or services, all the details have to be worked out, from developing a business strategy to finding investors for financing R&D. In short, if you've got a great idea, you can't just let it go out to the market naked as the day it was born: You've got to put some pants on it.

Ideas That Need Pants

These may be cool ideas, but development details need to be worked out before they can hit the market:

- The flying car
- Luxury condominiums on the moon
- Luxury condominiums on the sun
- Personal jet pack like the hero in *The Rocketeer*
- An inflatable doll that can hold a decent conversation

P

PUTTING WOOD BEHIND THE ARROW

Eggs in One Basket

When a company narrows its focus to one product, it is said to put all its wood behind one arrow. Sounds good—if the product doesn't flop. Just take a look at some of these terrible products and you'll see why sometimes it's best to keep a few arrows in your quiver.

⌐ - -{ **WHAT IT MEANS:**
To provide a company or product with capital and other resources

Worst Products Ever

Windows Millennium Edition (Me)

Unquestionably, Me is the worst version of Windows ever released. Shortly after hitting the streets in late 2000, users began reporting problems installing it, running it, using it with other programs and devices, and even stopping it from running. Aside from that, Me was just fine. Luckily for Microsoft shareholders, the company has a monopoly in the operating systems market, so users just went back to good ol' Windows 98.

DigiScent iSmell

During the dot-com boom, people were so crazy that some thought the Internet should smell like something. Imagine not only being assaulted by horrible sounds, pop-ups, and flashing ads, but also nasty electronic aromas. Luckily people didn't go for iSmell. Its name could have something to do with it.

Furby

Though this ugly, talking monster was wildly successful, it must have been a fluke. Tiger Electronics' investors should have lost wild sums of money and the company's management should be unemployed. After the Furby's launch in Christmas 1998, the thing was a must-have item. This speaks to the wackiness of the American public. See HERD INVESTMENT.

QCD

- - - - - - - - - - - - - - - - - - - -

Time of Reckoning

Imagine if you had to pay the government not just every April 15, but on January 15, July 15, and October 15. Yuck! If that's not bad enough,

the end of the quarter also marks the time when executives have to stand accountable to investors and the board of directors. If everything is going peachy in the business, these times just bring more work. If something's amiss, however, fat salaries, a company car, and bonuses are on the line.

Quarters are a big deal to executives because quarterly reports are often how investors decide whether or not to invest in a company. When investing in a company, an investor wants to see it grow over time. Looking at the financials only once a year isn't enough at all, so the company files reports every quarter.

Q3 FY06

As you may or may not know, this is how a big shot would say: "The third quarter of fiscal year 2006." This could mean the quarter that ends on September 30, 2006, but it also could mean the end of any other month of the year. Corporations can pick their fiscal year to end in any month. Generally, they pick a month in which they expect business to be slow. This will give them plenty of time to work (or cook) the books.

Strangest Year Ends

30 Brumaire

February 29

Stardate 23859.7

A Piece of the Pie

Quarters also mark the time when companies pay dividends. Dividends may be cash, stock, or property, although it's usually cash. Most secure and stable companies offer dividends to their stockholders, and their stock prices don't tend to move too wildly. High-growth companies, on the other hand, rarely offer dividends because their profits are all reinvested into the company to help maintain the growth.

RED-CHIP

WHAT IT MEANS:
The stock of a publicly traded Chinese company

China: In the Black

Writing a business book without mentioning China today is like ordering sweet pork without the sour. You just shouldn't get away with it.

Historians have dubbed the twentieth century "the American Century," and for good reason. The 100-year period witnessed America's rise from a growing manufacturing power to the world's only remaining superpower, dwarfing all other countries in both economic and military influence. But it might not last. Those same historians have now turned to predicting the future, claiming that the twenty-first century will go to China, a nation that has experienced the kind of record growth that economists have wet dreams about.

Investors in the United States and Europe have long since been aware of the giant panda in the room. Many of them have made a fortune on Chinese stocks. A takeoff on America's blue-chips (which describe the biggest U.S. companies—Wal-Mart, Ford, G.E., etc.), the red-chips offer investors a chance to directly participate in the great China growth story—and get rich doing it.

OTHER "CHIPS"

- **Pink-chips:** Girly stocks like cosmetic and fashion companies
- **Brown-chips:** Sanitation and sewage companies
- **Mafia-chips:** Cement contracting and casinos
- **Sin-chips:** Booze, cigarettes, strip clubs, etc.
- **Fat-chips:** Fast-food restaurants, snack foods, and Wal-Mart
- **Green-chips:** Eco-friendly companies
- **Corn-chips:** Midwestern U.S., Mexican, and Central American companies
- **Gray-chips:** Adult diaper companies, assisted living housing, and medical companies
- **Black-chips:** Funeral homes, cemeteries, and coffin manufacturing companies
- **Potato-chips:** Companies from Idaho

RELIGION STOCK

Stairway to Profits

Religion stock is a misleading term. It's not what you think. It doesn't refer to purchasing stock in a reli-

WHAT IT MEANS:
A stock that investors believe will continue to rise over the long term

gious faith and institution like the Catholic Church—too bad, you would have made a bundle. Nope, it refers to the stock of a company that investors blindly follow, believing that, as if under special protection from God himself, the shares will unquestionably continue to climb.

Like any religion, religion stocks are followed not just based on adherence to some sort of fundamental doctrine. This doctrine is called *investment fundamentals,* such as earnings growth, rising revenues, solid cash flow, and good, smart management.

Religions to Invest In

If you could buy stock in a religious faith, here are some of the organized religions in which you would have made quite a profit:

- **The Catholic Church:** Had some tough times during the Reformation, but it bounced back significantly during colonization, and is now the classic blue-chip faith.
- **The Mormons:** A century and a half ago they were wandering through the desert, persecuted for their faith. Today, they own Blockbuster and many other businesses. What's more, they're right at your doorstep every other day. Talk about good investor relations.
- **Islam:** Talk about a growth religion. For over 1,000 years, followers have multiplied into billions. Now that's explosive growth.
- **The Jews:** Though a persecuted small-cap, this religious group has managed to thrive in many different cultures throughout its 5,000-year history. It's had trouble finding solid partnerships, and was seriously hampered by Spanish secret short-sellers during the Inquisition. Other setbacks include the murdering of 6 million followers sixty years ago. The movie business, book publishing (have to be careful here), and law firms have helped keep their shares steadily climbing.

- **Evangelicals:** Look how well George W. Bush has done for himself. (Notice I said himself, not the country.)

REP SURFING

- -

Let Me Talk to Your Manager

WHAT IT MEANS:

With the click of a button, a customer service rep could save you hundreds of dollars by simply bending the rules a tiny bit. Remember these five tips:

Calling a customer service line until you get a representative who is willing to give you what you want

1. Try to gain the sympathy of the rep. Go ahead and give him a brief explanation of why you need his help.
2. Remind her of how long you've been a customer. While the rep probably doesn't care, it will make a more convincing case to her supervisor if she's questioned.
3. He's not the one fining you. It's the company's policy. So don't accuse him of doing anything. (Say, "Company X charged me," not, "You charged me.")
4. Call in the middle of the night. If there's a lighter call load, the rep might be more laid back and willing to help you.
5. Try to stay off the company's radar until you've given up on this strategy. Until then, don't yell, don't scream, and don't ask for the manager. Once they note that you're a raving lunatic, your chances will only get worse.

Note: But yelling and screaming might work too, especially in retail stores, where they are fearful you'll frighten other customers.

RETAIL LEAKAGE

If You Build it, They Will Shop

People need to shop. They need food, clothes, toilet paper, all kinds of things. But people also want to shop. We like owning stuff. It makes us feel like part of society. A cool new store will lure people out of their city or county and over to the next. Point is, when local demand for a specific product is not being met within a community, consumers are going to take their money elsewhere.

Some chain stores have high leakage rates from the transfer of revenue to corporate headquarters. But at least they pay employees and rent. With the Internet, bargain-basement prices and the latest trends are available to everyone with a library card and a credit card. If Smith County doesn't have Prada or Hustler shops and you want Prada and Hustler gear, the Internet can get them to you in no time. Some say, "Poor local retailers." We say, "That's what happens to dinosaurs."

✚ FIRST COINED: "Chadron Studies Mall Proposal to Create Ag Shopping Center," *Omaha World-Herald,* February 1984.

RETIREMENT PANIC

Do the Math

If you think you're a little short, you could do any of these things:

WHAT IT MEANS:
Fear that you may not have enough money for retirement

Work another year or two, eat dog food for breakfast, or take up smoking. Of course, the best advice is to start saving early. Retirement advisors have shown us how a MacDonald's employee can become a millionaire at fifty-five by investing a few bucks a paycheck twice a month beginning at age fourteen. While four decades in a MacDonald's isn't exactly the American Dream, it's one way to wealth as long as you keep your expenses down.

Movin' on Down

Another interesting phenomenon is the sell-the-house-and-move-to-Mississippi plan. When moving from the more expensive states, this can add a few hundred grand to your nest egg, though you might not see your kids again. (This may or may not be an upside.) While some are moving to cheaper states, others are moving to cheaper countries. Mexico has long been an attractive destination for American retirees, while Spain has been big for the Brits. If you're up for a real adventure in your golden years, try Cambodia or the Congo. You can buy an entire town for less than the price of your high-definition television. Of course, HDTV probably offers a more pleasant overall experience.

Conventional wisdom holds that after you retire, you can pull around 7 percent out of your portfolio every year. Some say that that number is too high and 4 percent is closer. Either way, to be able to spend $50,000 a year, you'd need around a million bucks in your portfolio. Start saving.

✚ **FIRST COINED:** Linda Stern, "The Golden Fears," *Newsweek,* November 1997.

RIGHTSIZING

Layoff or Rightoff?

You know the stories: Your company grew too quickly; market conditions changed; there was a general economic slowdown. Point is, you're fired.

But everything needs to be spun. In this world of euphemisms, where people with mental retardation are "special" and disabled people are "physically challenged," it's not hard to imagine that your company "rightsized" and you just "lost" your job.

Rightshore?

Part of rightsizing can be moving some of the jobs overseas, that is, restructuring a company's workforce to access the best possible mix of local and overseas talent.

Rightshoring is a term trademarked by Capgemini. According to the company's Web site, their approach "cuts across geographies to access the right IT service, in the right place and at the right price." This should save a business "20 to 50 percent compared to the cost of doing business onshore."

The economic reason for a business to Rightshore or even offshore is to reduce costs. Not only does this obviously benefit the company, it benefits the countries and the consumers as well. Because the products are cheaper across the board, everyone wins—or so goes the theory of free-trade economics that we live by.

✚ **FIRST COINED:** John H. Sheridan, "A Matter of Perspective," *Industry Week,* January 1988.

RIO HEDGE

Trading Dangerously

Traders win and lose millions every day. It's a risky business. Just as many of them fly high in riches, many get sunk. Maybe cement shoes sunk, maybe federal penitentiary sunk, or maybe just bankruptcy sunk, but sunk.

WHAT IT MEANS:

When a losing trader makes one last trade and hedges his or her bet by buying a one-way ticket to Rio de Janeiro or some other exotic, distant place

To Hedge or Not to Hedge?

The idea of a "hedge" is to prevent a complete loss of a bet by betting an additional amount against the original wager. A good example of this is insurance in blackjack.

Insurance is something you can buy if the dealer's up-card is an ace. You would do this because if the face-down card gives the dealer blackjack, you only end up losing half your original bet. The hedge also reduces your gains because you're betting against yourself.

The Rio hedge version of insurance is a suitcase full of cash and a plane ticket.

So, if your last trade *is* a winner, the only thing you lose on the bet is the plane ticket (which may or may not be refundable).

ROACH BAIT

Marketers Make the World Go Round

Marketers think we're lemmings. All they need to do is convince a couple of us to buy their garbage, and then hordes of us will follow

WHAT IT MEANS:

A marketing campaign in which a socially adept person, a roacher, is hired to promote a product by posing as a regular person

161

suit. With the roach bait technique, instead of convincing us of anything, they hire someone to pretend to be convinced in public. Then, they want us all to jump off the cliff.

To Marketers, My Dear, You're But a Cockroach

Roach bait is a pretty disgusting term if you think about what the stuff does. The term comes from poison applied to roach-infested areas. The idea is that a cockroach eats the bait, returns to its nest and excretes feces that are contaminated with the poison. The original roach dies, but other roaches eat the contaminated feces, and the killing cycle continues.

Now, put this into a marketing scenario: After a consumer is infected with the marketing ideas, he spreads the virus to his family and friends.

The idea behind the roach-bait technique is to get people talking about the product, spreading its benefits by word of mouth. If the ploy fails, however, consumers have only bad things to say.

Viral Marketing

Roach bait falls into the broader category of viral marketing, promoting a service or product by getting existing customers to pass along a marketing pitch to friends, family, and colleagues.

Famous Viral Campaigns

By only allowing existing users to give accounts to others, Gmail spread through the Internet like a wildfire. For my first Gmail account, I paid an Iranian girl $5. Now I have eighty-three accounts, all of which I got for free.

Borat: Our Kazakh friend's presence on MySpace.com was another very successful virus. By placing his picture on your front page, you could get free tickets to his premieres. Now, everyone knows what *Yegshamesh* means.

The campaign for the animated movie *Aqua Teen Hunger Force* was treated as a terror threat by Boston authorities, virtually shutting down the city in fear that the Mooninite figures scattered around were bombs. They weren't bombs; they were essentially homemade Lite-Brites. (That this occurred in Boston, home to Harvard, MIT, and other famous schools of learning, is embarrassing.)

SCREENSUCKING

Idle Eyes Are the Devil's . . .

WHAT IT MEANS: Wasting time sitting in front of a screen

With everything vying for our attention, it's not surprising that we spend so much time with our eyes glued to something. Screensucking is a concept that will sadly hit close to home for many of us. If you spend hours in front of the boob tube, a computer, or video games, you're spending your time screensucking. Sure, there are a few television programs worth watching—I can count two—but isn't it much nicer to sit and read an intelligently written, topical, and hard-hitting book?

ACCEPTABLE REASONS TO SCREENSUCK
- Serious illness
- Serious leg injury
- Surgery recovery
- In prison
- Hung over
- Under twelve on a snow day

SEAGULL MANAGER

Oh, Shoot!

Colorfully described as "a manager who flies in, makes a lot of noise, [defecates] all over everything, then leaves," in *Wired* magazine.

'Nough said.

WHAT IT MEANS:
A manager who interacts with employees only to criticize their work or when a problem arises

➕ **FIRST COINED:** Michael Madison, "The Sharp End," *Marketing*, May 1988.

SERVER FARM

A Very Fat Farm

The idea of a server farm is to better organize computer processes by distributing the workload evenly between the individual servers. Similar to a power plant, a server farm relies on load-balancing to track demand for processing power and prioritize tasks. When one server in a farm fails, another can step in and do the work.

WHAT IT MEANS:
A large group of Internet servers at a single location

Moogle

Big businesses, especially large high-tech and Internet firms, need big servers. Google, one of the biggest Internet companies in the world, is estimated to have 450,000 servers.

SHORT SELLING

Betting with the House

WHAT IT MEANS:
Borrowing a security, selling it, and replacing it at a later date

While most stock market bets go long on an investment, expecting that the price will rise, selling short expects the opposite to happen. Short sellers make money when the stock price goes down because they borrow a security (typically from their broker) and sell it. If the price decreases, the short seller can buy the stock back at a cheaper price, and return it. If the price goes up, the short seller must buy the stock at a higher price and return it.

Short Selling 101

Let's say you want to short 100 shares of Stockbomb.com, which is valued at $10 per share. What you would do is borrow 100 shares of the company and then immediately sell those shares for a total of $1000. If the price of Stockbomb.com shares later falls to $8 per share, you could then buy 100 shares back for $800, return the shares to their original owner, and make a $200 profit. Short selling can also lose. If the price of Stockbomb.com goes up to $12 per share, you could buy back the shares for $1,200 and return them to the owner, and lose $200.

Short selling has the potential for unlimited losses. If, for example, the shares of Stockbomb.com went up to $100 per share, you would have to buy them for $10,000, a loss of $9000. Or if it went up to $100,000 per share, you'd owe $10 million. In going long, losses are limited, but gains are unlimited. That is, the price can only go down to zero but could go up to infinity. In short selling, it's the opposite because the higher the price goes, the more you lose. So, short carefully.

A Short History

Short selling has been seen as a shady business since at least the eighteenth century, when England banned it. Short sellers are usually looked upon with suspicion because people believe that they profit from the misfortune of others, like the hedge betters at a craps table. Many academic studies, however, have claimed that short-selling makes an important contribution to stock market efficiency.

Less than 5 percent of all short selling is done by public investors and traders. This means that 95 percent of the deals are done by broker-dealers and market makers—people who, supposedly, know their stuff.

Nudity in the Market

Naked short selling is when you short a stock without first borrowing it. The risk is that you might not be able to get the stocks when you need to deliver on the sale. With Regulation SHO, the SEC is attempting to reduce the number of potential failures to deliver for naked short selling deals by limiting the time in which a broker can permit failures to deliver.

SINGLE-DIGIT MIDGET

Finally, a Stock I Can Afford

WHAT IT MEANS:
A stock priced below $10

Little companies aren't all bad. Sometimes they turn into big companies, and if you bought them while they were single-digit midgets, you could be set. However, even penny stocks can be expensive if they drop significantly. Some companies trade for under a buck. Others trade for over a grand. The price alone doesn't mean one is a good deal and the other isn't. Remember that just because a stock sells for less than a Happy Meal doesn't mean it's a good buy.

If you buy $1000 worth of stock for a dime, or one stock for $1000, if the stock drops 90 percent, you lose the same amount in both cases. Don't be seduced by the relative cheapness of the dime stock. A stock that is valued at a dime is much easier for stock sharks to manipulate according to their interests, which may not be in line with yours.

The Next Microsoft

You've probably heard someone say about a cheap stock, "Microsoft had to start somewhere." In point of fact, Microsoft was never a single-digit midget. It went public at $21 in 1986 and now trades around $30. But this doesn't mean you'd have only made a few bucks. The stock has split so many times that if you bought only one share at the IPO price, today you'd own 288 shares, each having paid $4.19 in dividends. That's almost $10,000 altogether. Even the janitor who received 100 shares back then is now a millionaire. (See, there's still hope for that nephew of yours yet.)

SKILL OBSOLESCENCE

What Happened to All Those Typesetters?

As economies change, once-important skills and occupations become

> WHAT IT MEANS:
>
> An occupation or skill that has become replaced by technology

obsolete and ultimately vanish into obscurity. Today, with more and more manufacturing jobs going overseas or being replaced by new technologies, many Americans find that the skills they possess are no longer marketable. Adult retraining programs and other educational services are often recommended to retrain these workers to find employment in the New Economy.

But it isn't just blue-collar workers that are at risk. After the terrorist attacks of September 11, the dot-com bust, and corporate scandals like Enron ravaged the nation, there was no longer the kind of need for securities research analysts as there once was. With the passing of Sarbanes Oxley, and through the vigilant efforts of New York City Attorney General Elliot Spitzer, times in the research business are a-changing. As an example, firms like UBS Paine Webber used to employ around 4,000 research analysts. Today, they boast a few hundred.

Now, if we could only find a way to replace all those damned attorneys . . .

What should I know?

You can't predict the future completely, but you can get an idea about what skills will be marketable in the future and what will not.

Languages to Know

With the Chinese economy growing at a rate of around 10 percent annually for over a decade, speaking Mandarin Chinese will be a great asset to the young enterprising businessperson.

Languages to Avoid

Don't bother studying Aramaic. It's a dead language and, at best, it could land you in a Mel Gibson film. Also, if you plan on living in the Southwest United States, English is becoming increasingly irrelevant.

Technologies to Know

Not surprisingly, computers are the way to go. Learn as much about them as you can.

Technologies to Avoid

Knowledge of these technologies is utterly useless:

- The abacus
- The telegraph
- The VCR
- Last year's PC

Occupations to Enter

There will never be a shortage of DMV workers. Even if they *could* be replaced by robots, no technology would be able to replicate the polite, caring service that they provide.

Occupations to Avoid

Steel and automotive manufacturing. (Also, grave digging—mainly because it's just creepy.)

SLAMMING

Phone Companies Are the Anti-Christ

WHAT IT MEANS:
Changing a customer's service provider without their permission

It's 6 P.M. and you're just sitting down to have dinner after a long day at the office. You take your first sip of wine, sit back in your chair, and exhale all the stress that accompanies the modern way of life. Then, right when you feel that life really isn't that horrible and that maybe, just maybe you can stand one more day of looking at your boss's weasel face, inevitably, the phone rings. Who is it? Why, a telemarketer advertising some stupid phone company plan, of course. So what do you do? You slam the phone down, hoping never to hear from them again. But, you may not have heard the last of them. Worse than calling back, they might just slam you!

Slamming and telephone fraud have been around since the first ring. However, slamming became more visible ever since the deregulation of the telecommunications industry in the mid-1980s, when companies like AT&T split up into local and long-distance carriers. As a result, local carriers became responsible for distributing telephone numbers to customers.

The most common kind of slamming is when a telemarketer decides to submit an order to change the victim's carrier without their consent. But there are other kinds, including a clever scam that involves a fraudulent survey or contest. In this scenario, the participant is unaware that the small print on their entry is an authorization to switch their telephone service to another carrier.

Banning Slamming

After repeated complaints from customers, federal and state legislative action has been taken to combat slamming. There is currently an industry-wide FCC requirement that requires all changes in a residential customer's local, local toll, and long distance service to be verified in one of the following ways before the change is made: by the customer's written signature on a form, by an independent third party, or by electronic authorization that requires a consumer to call in from the phone on which the service is to be changed.

Also, most large companies and local carriers have set up anti-slamming customer service centers. Customers are now able to freeze their account if they suspect they've been slammed.

➕ **FIRST COINED:** Mark A. Kellner, "AT&T to Investigate 'Slamming' Cases," *MIS Week,* December 1988.

SLEEPER

Snoozy Stocks

Sleeper stocks are good buys. They're underpriced because of their lack of exposure rather than their fundamentals.

It may take a quarterly report, an exciting announcement, or a new product, but one thing is for certain. At the right moment, they will awake. Not from either a rooster or an alarm clock, of course, but from a hedge fund, an institution, or deep-pocketed investor.

SLEEPING BEAUTY

Wake up, My Darling. I Need Some Assets!

Like the name suggests, a sleeping beauty is attractive, often possess-

ing particularly sexy features such as a large amount of cash, undervalued real estate, or an exciting product. One of the best examples of a great sleeping beauty is the fictitious New England Wire & Cable in the clever comedy *Other People's Money* (1991) starring Danny DeVito.

DeVito plays Larry the Liquidator, a hostile takeover shark always looking for his next victim. One morning, his computer tells him that the "fairest of them all" is New England Wire & Cable, a company that has been the center of a small town's economic life for generations. But Larry the Liquidator doesn't care about that. He cares that the company's stock has plummeted and that its book value is now higher than the price of its stock. Viewing the future of the wire-and-cable industry to be bleak considering new technologies such as fiber optics, Larry's plan is take over the company, fire everyone, and sell off its assets. In the end, Larry successfully takes over the company, falls in love with the company president's daughter, and sells the factory to the Japanese to make air bags, putting everyone back to work.

Real-life sleeping beauties can be awakened either harshly or gently, the target of either a friendly merger or a hostile takeover.

SOUL PROPRIETOR

Praise Jesus . . . Now Let's Make Cash

WHAT IT MEANS:
A businessperson who balances work with emotional and spiritual growth

The marriage of religion and entrepreneurship isn't new. For some faiths, fortune favors the faithful. This prosperity theology is common in many protestant sects, which claim that God wants Christians to be successful in every way, including financially. This is certainly a more saleable dogma than the Catholic version, in which God wants you to suffer in every way, including financially. And also better than the Jewish version, where God wants you to suffer in every way . . . excluding financially.

SPAMMIFIED

Spammity Spam, Wonderful Spam

WHAT IT MEANS:
When a legitimate e-mail ends up in the spam folder

Despite the filters on most e-mail servers, e-mails hyping toilet stocks, selling Viagra, and claiming that you've won the Dutch lottery show up in your inbox every day. Filters, in an effort to catch these elusive e-mails, occasionally grab e-mails that have little to do with stocks, penises, or the Low Countries and spammify notes from your mother or your spouse into the junk-mail bin.

But spammification also has its benefits. It can be used as an excuse for not responding to e-mails in a timely manner.

The Growth of Spam

Spam has grown like kudzu over the past several years. In 2005, there were about 30 billion per day. In 2006, there were 55 billion. In early 2007, there were about 90 billion per day. That means that each of the billion or so people on the Internet was receiving about ninety spam messages a day.

Work Spam

Those paper pushers upstairs are lazy. Instead of figuring out to whom to send information, they just blast their whole contact list with their garbage, increasing your spam load by about 30 percent. You're not involved in the executive dinners, the press conferences, management's adventure vacations, or any of the other hundreds, if not thousands, of garbage e-mails you receive.

While the e-mails they send you aren't relevant or interesting, it's not quite spam either (even though it feels like it). Spam must be unsolicited and bulk, but since you work for these clowns and it goes to your work e-mail address, they can send you any piece of garbage they want. Luckily, you can just spammify the junk.

You Think That's Bad?

All in all, it's not too difficult to check your spam folder. Unless, of course, you're like Microsoft's Bill Gates, who reportedly gets over 4 million pieces of spam daily and has an entire department of e-mail deleters to filter through his mail. If a person can delete sixty spam messages per minute, Bill Gates's e-mail would require over 1,000 man-hours of work per day. And, if they're low-end techies, and you can pay them $15 per hour, you have a spam staff budget of $15,000 per day. Now you see why MS Office is so expensive and why spam is the devil.

SPAVE

The More You Buy, the More You Save!

This little word is a portmanteau of *spend* and *save*. There are two

WHAT IT MEANS:
To spend money on items priced below normal retail cost, saving the difference

types of spavers in this world. The first are just smart shoppers, who recognize a good deal when why see one, and only buy the products they need.

The other type of spaver is a little more obsessive. They've got a problem buying things just because they've found a good deal, even if they don't need the product. This spaver ends up with a garage full of lamps, knickknacks, and expired cans of garbanzo beans. As far as the wallet goes, that's empty.

➕ **FIRST COINED:** Adrienne T. Washington, "Beach Means Rejuvenation for Everyone," *Washington Times,* May 1996.

STAG

Neither Bull nor Bear

Stags are a special kind of Wall Street animal. They believe that IPOs have nowhere to go but up. But just as with both bulls and bears, any idea

WHAT IT MEANS:
An investor who purchases shares in an IPO with the intention of quickly selling them after the price has risen

about the market can bite you in the behind. Hard.

IPOs usually generate a fair amount of publicity, especially as they become increasingly rare as reverse mergers become

174

mainstream. The main purpose of an IPO is to raise capital for the corporation. While IPOs are effective at raising capital, being listed on a stock exchange takes a lot of time and money and imposes heavy regulatory compliance and reporting requirements.

But even with all that, IPOs can still flop. One of the worst in history occurred in 2006 with the company Vonage. Its initial offering of $17 hit $8 at the end of the year, and was floating in the $3 range in March, 2007. Stag soup anyone?

SUNLIGHTING

Step into the Sunlight!

We're not suckers. We know that there's precious little time in life

> **WHAT IT MEANS:**
> Doing paid work while taking time away from your day job

for the things that really matter. Spend more time with the kids, sleep eight hours a day, and spend more time watching reruns of *Friends*. How do you do this? Do your personal work at your nine to five.

This is especially good advice if you see your day job as something to make ends meet while you pursue some other endeavor. And if that endeavor is the work you do while sunlighting, then all the more power to you . . . until you get caught.

Melanoma?

Of course, there can be negative repercussions. As you probably know, your network administrator can see what Web sites you visit and, on occasion, can see every little word you type into your computer. Be careful. Make friends with them, even have an affair if you must.

Also, this book was largely written while sunlighting. I had to commit unspeakable acts with my network administrator. Tell no one.

➕ **FIRST COINED:** John Darnton, "Madrid's New Working Class: The Bureaucrats," *New York Times,* February 1983.

SWEAT EQUITY

Sweating for a Dream

{ **WHAT IT MEANS:**

Equity earned through working for a business

Sweat equity does not refer to risky investments, that is, how much you sweat while anxiously awaiting the market's opening and closing bells to find out how much you've made or lost.

Rather, it's the amount of equity you've built up in a business directly through your labor. For example, say you've worked fourteen-hour days to start up your dream funeral home, but your partner hasn't worked even one. (She's supplied all of your seed money, though.) The partner does not own 100 percent of the business just because she put up 100 percent of the capital; you, too, own a part. You earned a portion of the equity through your hard work. Assuming you're not a chump and got everything in writing.

Examples of How You Can Earn Sweat Equity

You work at a small startup called Poogle, and your boss can't afford to pay you. Instead of salary, you negotiate a 10 percent share in the business. Fast forward ten years, and either you're a millionaire or you're homeless.

Your wife wants to fix up the house before you sell it. In order to maximize profits, you agree to tile the kitchen yourself. So you spend four weekends in a row slaving over the floor to increase the value and avoid labor costs. Your wife is pleased. She thanks you by taking your sweat equity and buying herself a diamond tennis bracelet.

TECHNO-STRIKE

I'm a Fire Starter, Twisted Fire Starter

The Internet, we are learning, is a huge can of worms. Sure, there's great stuff on it, like news, forums where we can chat with friends and associates, shopping, amazing amounts of accessible research, places to buy flowers for your sweetie and, of course, hard-core pornography of all kinds. But there are also nasty things like e-mail bombs, viruses, pop-ups, and spam, the scourge of the Internet.

WHAT IT MEANS:

A labor action in which union members overload a company with e-mail messages, faxes, and Web site hits in an effort to shut down the electronic part of the company's business

➕ **FIRST COINED:** Barrie Clement, "Flying Pickets on the Superhighway," *The Independent,* February 1998.

TEN BAGGER

That's a Load of Cash!

Not to be confused with a ten bag (a.k.a. dime bag), which is $10 worth of marijuana, this expression was coined by Peter Lynch, one of the greatest and funniest investors of all time, in his book, *One Up on Wall Street* (1989).

WHAT IT MEANS:

An investment that's worth ten times the price you paid for it

FIVE GREAT PETER LYNCH QUOTES

1. "If all the economists in the world were laid end to end, it wouldn't be a bad thing."
2. "Everyone has the brainpower to follow the stock market. If you made it through fifth-grade math, you can do it."

3. "The key to making money in stocks is not to get scared out of them."

4. "Although it's easy to forget sometimes, a share is not a lottery ticket . . . it's part-ownership of a business."

5. "Go for a business that any idiot can run—because sooner or later, any idiot probably is going to run it."

TGIM

Just Another Marvelous Monday

{ **WHAT IT MEANS:** An acronym for "thank God it's Monday"

Few people experience this feeling of elatedness when they drag their sleepy bodies to work on Monday after a long weekend. A play on TGIF, TGIM affects only two kinds of people: the really, really nerdy, or the really, really, lonely. Sociopathic managers who take pleasure in berating employees might also enjoy the occasional TGIM feeling.

Ways to Experience TGIM

Here are a few things to try that might make you shout, "TGIM!":

- Have a shitty weekend.
- Become a strip-club owner.
- Stay home until Tuesday.
- Spend Sunday with your in-laws.
- Become king . . . or queen.
- Win the lottery Monday morning.
- Realize it's filet mignon day in the cafeteria.
- Hear that your boss has suddenly fallen ill. She is not expected back soon, if ever.

➕ **FIRST COINED**: Robert L. Miller, "Letter from the Publisher," *Sports Illustrated,* May 1984.

THROW IT OVER THE WALL

The Buck Stops . . . over There

┌─ **WHAT IT MEANS**:
Passing a project or problem to another person or department

Sometime when a project is so difficult, so confounding, so seemingly impossible, the best thing to do is make it someone else's problem. Yep, send it off to the next sucker. After all, you're not just a small cog in the capitalist machine; you're also a small cog in your company. So pass the buck and take a long lunch. Tomorrow's another day.

➕ **FIRST COINED**: Philip Siekman, "Cessna Tackles Lean Manufacturing," *Fortune,* May 2000.

TICKER SHOCK

That Sinking Feeling

┌─ **WHAT IT MEANS**:
The agony investors feel when the stock market drops and the value of their portfolio diminishes

People feel losses much more strongly than they do gains. So, if a portfolio goes up 70 percent zZand later drops 20 percent, they feel like net losers even though that's not the case at all. This is true for feelings in other aspects of life too. As a younger man, I recall the agony I felt when one of my five girlfriends left me. Torture! But, now I see I was a net winner. Still up 80 percent. Not bad at all.

It's the Stock Market, Stupid

Never forget that stock markets move up and down; they can explode and implode. Over the long term, the general trend is up. Trying to beat that trend is difficult, but it's not exactly a crap shoot either. In fact, on average, gamblers lose ten cents per dollar bet, while investors, on average, win ten cents per dollar invested per year. Of course, you can still lose your shirt if you pick wrong stock, just as you would if you picked the wrong slot machine. Spread out your bets, however, and, over time, you'll come out a winner—unlike in Las Vegas.

Trade Rage

There are riskier and safer investments, just like "red" is a safer bet than "00." Some have gone insane after experiencing ticker shock . . . like Mark Barton.

In 1999, Barton shot and killed nine people and injured thirteen more at two day trading firms in Atlanta, Georgia. Barton, a day trader, is believed to have been motivated by $105,000 in losses over the previous two months. After the shooting, Barton committed suicide at a gas station, having been spotted by police.

Following the shootings, police found that Barton's second wife and two children had been murdered by hammer blows a few days before. The children had then been placed in bed, as if sleeping.

TRAILING SPOUSE

Benefits of Being Number Two

Sure, you're second when it comes to money and prestige, but it's not all gloom and doom. While your spouse is working late, you get to watch television, read, take walks, and even have an affair. Your spouse pays for your car, your haircuts, your manicures, and you get to enjoy life's finest pleasure: free time.

But not all trailing spouses are content with sitting on their duff. Consider these famous trailing spouses:

- Hillary Clinton
- Bill Clinton
- Minnie Mouse
- Ricky Ricardo
- Siegfried Fischbacher (of Siegfried and Roy)
- Chewbacca the Wookie

➕ **FIRST COINED:** "Firms Transferring Employees Often Find Jobs for Spouses," *Wall Street Journal,* January 1982.

TRIPLE BOTTOM LINE

Zero Carbon Footprint, Fair Trade, and Losing $10 Million per Quarter

A company could save every panda, condor, and elephant in the world, but unless there's a profitable business model, it will sink.

However, flogging employees for being late and throwing trash off the Santa Monica Pier isn't a great plan either, despite the few dollars it saves. Not that I would know of such a company.

TROLLEYOLOGY

What You Got in There?

You don't have to dig through someone's garbage can to find out more about them. You can just follow them around the aisles of the

WHAT IT MEANS: The study of the correlation between the contents of a person's shopping cart (trolley) and that person's personality

local grocery store. While generic brands are a sure sign that someone is either poor or cheap, other items are more difficult to interpret. But if you can, you might just find the person you've been looking for. Allow me to help you find romance between the deli and the dried fruits.

Food	Interpretation
Eggs	Morning person
Wonder Bread	Bland
Clamato	Lives with or shops for grandma
Green tea	Health-crazed socialist
Doritos	See DORITO SYNDROME
Brie	Doesn't shave
Tomato soup	Simple
Wine	Faux sophisticate
Dried fruits	Constipated
Beans	Gassy
Candy	Parent or child molester
Corn tortillas	Likes Frisbee

➕ **FIRST COINED:** Samm Taylor, "Shopped by Your Trolley," *The Mirror,* January 1997.

TWEEDS TO RICHES

The Millionaire Professor

┗ ─ ─ { **WHAT IT MEANS:**
University professors or graduate students who take their research and parlay it into a successful company

Sometimes, the ivory tower becomes no fun. Not enough money for fancy cars, but too much money to take risks. Once in a great while, a professor's research will pay off financially. These academics usually teach chemistry or computer science, not history or philosophy. Humanists are screwed. Didn't they teach you that in college?

TWO COMMAS

It's All About the Benjamins

┗ ─ ─ { **WHAT IT MEANS:**
A million dollars

There are more slang words for money than anything except for sex and alcohol. And since you might need money to get the other two, here's a list of terms to make you sound rich at least.

TERMS FOR MONEY

- Bacon
- Bucks
- Cash
- Cheddar
- Dead presidents
- Dough
- Ducats
- Flow
- Frogskins
- Greenbacks
- Grip
- Loot

- Moolah
- Simoleons
- Wad
- $5 bill: Five spot
- $20 bill: Jackson
- $50 bill: Grant
- $100 bill: Bill, Benjamin, C-note

UNDERWATER OPTIONS

No Options

WHAT IT MEANS:
Stock options that are more expensive than the current market price of the stock

If you joined a company while its stock price was inflated, and you're working for options, when the price falls, your options are worthless. Exercising these options would allow you to buy high and sell low. And for those of you who haven't taken Finance 101, that's exactly what you don't want to do.

Stock options are privileges that give the buyer the right, but not the obligation, to buy or sell a stock at an agreed-upon price within a certain period or on a specific date.

UNHIRABLES

Not All That Admirable

WHAT IT MEANS:
Employees who cannot leave their current company because they would lose a large portfolio of unvested stock options

Although unhirables can't be convinced to defect, their reasons are not similar to Eliot Ness and his band of lawmen. Though the untouchables were incorruptible for moral reasons, unhirables don't leave their jobs for financial concerns. So they are, in fact, hirable, just not for what anyone is willing to pay.

UNLOCK DATE

Lock Blocking

A company and its investment bank will enter into a lockup agreement so that shares owned by insiders don't enter the public market too soon after the IPO and send

the stock spiraling downward. This usually lasts for 180 days, although the period could be as short as three months and as long as three years.

If you're thinking like a STAG and want to invest in a company that's just had or is about to have an IPO, you'll want to know if that company has a lockup agreement and how long it lasts. This information is critical because a company's stock price could drop in anticipation of the lockup date, so you'll want to keep an eye on the price and the company's SEC filings. Remember that in most IPOs, a small percentage of the total outstanding shares are sold to the public. Insiders generally own most of them. If these insiders decide to dump large blocks of the stock on the market, it could have a negative impact on the price.

Insider Information

Many believe that if there's heavy selling after the lockup expiration, insiders must know something negative about the company that is making them ship. While that may be the case, it's far more likely that they just want some money to buy cars, houses, and different stocks.

C

UPSTAFF

The More the Merrier

WHAT IT MEANS: An increase in the size of a company's workforce

From pouring tap water into the water cooler to installing fans instead of A/C, some employers will do whatever they can to save the firm a buck or two. In this cost-cutting mission, they'll also try to squeeze whatever work they can get out of you. But with growth comes the need for more workers—no matter how thrifty an employer wants to be.

Time to Upstaff

If you own a business and are debating whether or not to upstaff, here are some classic signs that it's time to bite the bullet and spend the cash:

1. You have twice as many departments as employees to run them.
2. When you buy lunch for the staff on Friday, it costs around $5.
3. When someone calls the company, you answer.
4. You use a large mirror in the boardroom to give the appearance of more people.
5. Employee of the month has gone to the same worker for the last year and a half.
6. The only sexual harassment complaint ever filed was by your right hand. Repeatedly.
7. At the Christmas party, the only woman to flirt with is your wife.
8. You took everyone on a company field trip on your motorcycle.
9. The company directory system reads, "YOU: Ext. 101, ME: Ext. 102."

VANILLA

Not So Boring

WHAT IT MEANS: A straight-laced, conservative businessperson

In the business world, it's surprising how many executives, analysts, and bankers have been crack heads, cons, and pimps. Now, when these types, whether reformed or not, get in a pinch, you watch how fast they'll call in their RIO HEDGE, shred the documents, and burn down the factory. Lickety split.

The vanilla partner is the one who these dirt bags send in to do photo ops and whose name appears on the financial statements. He's not rocky road. He's not pralines and cream. He's not even chocolate. He's vanilla, plain and simple. Sure, he might not be that bright (he might even be clinically retarded), but he is the face and voice of the company. And he's not going to be on that plane to Rio. He won't help burn the factory down, either. He'll be asleep in his big home waiting for the feds to arrive, wondering how this could have ever happened. (Ironically, he's never once wondered how he could have risen to the top to begin with.)

VEAL PEN

Are You Tender Yet?

WHAT IT MEANS: A cubicle

Veal, as you probably know, is raised in crates that restrict physical movement in order to minimize the growth of tough muscle fiber and to keep the flesh white and tender. Yum.

You, on the other hand, are kept in a cubical for other reasons, but the effect is essentially the same.

Cubicle Life

A cubicle is a partially enclosed workspace, separated from neighboring workspaces by partitions, generally five to six feet high. Hades, as reported in Homer's *Odyssey*, looks exactly the same.

No work of fiction has exposed and elucidated cubicle life better than Scott Adams's *Dilbert* franchise. *Dilbert* portrays corporate culture and office life in a Kafkaesque manner. Bureaucracy exists for its own sake; office politics stand in the way of productivity; employees' skills and efforts are never rewarded.

> "The brain is a wonderful organ. It starts working the moment you get up in the morning and does not stop until you get into the office."
>
> *Robert Frost*

VENTURE CATALYST

Money Makes the World Go Round

WHAT IT MEANS:
A firm or person who obtains venture capital financing for new companies that wouldn't otherwise have access to venture capital

There's a lot of money out there, and a lot of rich people are looking to turn it into more money by investing in your company. But access is everything. Since you don't have the ear of these big shots, it might be tough. Enter the venture catalyst, who, through his or her connections, acquires the cash you need to grow . . . for a small percentage, of course.

VIATICAL SETTLEMENTS

A Grim Way to Reap Profits

A viatical settlement allows you to invest in another person's life insurance policy by buying it at a discount to its face value. Because

{ **WHAT IT MEANS:**

The purchase—at a discount—of a dying person's life insurance policy, which can be cashed in after the person's death

you collect the death benefit when the seller dies, your rate of return is determined by the seller's life expectancy and how long that person actually lives. Only in America.

If the seller dies before the expected date, you, the investor, make more money; if the person sticks it out for longer than expected, you make less money—and can even lose your shirt. If the person stubbornly lives long enough, you can even lose some of your principal if you have to pay additional premiums to maintain the policy. The nerve of some people.

A matter of life and death, viatical settlements are inherently risky, as there is no clear way to tell when your seller will finally kick the bucket. For this reason, the SEC warns that investors should "exercise caution and thoroughly investigate before you consider investing in a viatical settlement."

Many state insurance commissioners license the companies that buy viatical settlements to sell to investors. To find out who your state insurance regulator is, go to the National Association of Insurance Commissioners Web site at *www.naic.org*. For those of you who are terminally ill, the U.S. Federal Trade Commission also has information about how to sell your life insurance policy at *www.ftc.gov/opa/1995/12/via.htm*.

Picking a Good Viatical Settlement

While betting on death ain't easy, it can be done. Here are some tips to picking a seller of a viatical settlement:

- **Find out their religion.** Statistics show that devoted people live longer than non-believers. (Though atheists claim they live in the dark.)
- **Is the disease potentially curable?** Make sure there are no new treatment options or surgical techniques.
- **Interview the person or people they know.** What's their overall attitude? Do they seem like a fighter or not?
- **Bet on sure killers like rare diseases.** Stay away from certain forms of cancer and AIDS. Though deadly, they're very enigmatic and patient-specific when it comes to how long patients can tough it out.
- **Research doesn't have to be dull.** Watch entertaining and informative television shows like *House* and *Grey's Anatomy* to learn about some of the rarest and deadliest diseases that can make you rich.

VICE INVESTING

You Can Bet on Beer!

WHAT IT MEANS:
An investment strategy that targets companies selling products related to vices, such as alcohol, tobacco, and gambling

There's nothing that we Americans like more before we do anything fun or after we do anything stressful than drinking. Some may turn to a Bud after a hard day's work, others a glass of wine. Still others will down vodka like it's water. What it is doesn't really matter, as long as they keep drinking. You can always count on sin.

Do You Like Sin? (Circle Options If So)

1. Beer
2. Casinos
3. Cigarettes
4. Cigars
5. Mixed drinks
6. Pornography
7. Prostitutes
8. Strip clubs
9. Wine

While it seems difficult to legally invest in some of these, let's not kid ourselves about where your dollars end up when you invest in government bonds in Thailand or Nevada.

VOLUNTARY SIMPLICITY

Not Just Cheapskates

Not to be confused with frugality, voluntary simplicity is defined by

{ **WHAT IT MEANS:**

A lifestyle that shuns luxury, flamboyance, and pretense

wanting fewer things, not paying less for them. Forget money, gadgets, and brand names—get back to what matters: family, nature, and community. Also called simple living, people who practice this seek to find meaning in life outside consumerism, wealth, and Wal-Mart.

Basically, they're boring.

According to Linda Breen Pierce, founder of the Pierce Simplicity Study, these ten suggestions to simple living should be taken in small doses:

1. Don't let any material thing come into your home unless you absolutely love it and want to keep it until it is beyond repair.

2. Live in a home with only those rooms that you or someone in your family uses every day.

3. Limit your work (outside of the home) to thirty hours a week, twenty if you are a parent.

4. Select a home and place of employment no more than thirty minutes away from each other.

5. Limit your children's extracurricular activities to one to three a week, depending on age.

6. Take three to four months off every few years and go live in a foreign country.

7. Spend at least an hour a week in a natural setting, away from crowds of people, traffic, and buildings.

8. Do whatever you need to do to connect with a sense of spirit in your life, whether it be prayer, religious services, journal writing, meditation, or spiritually related reading.

9. Seek the support of others who want to simplify their lives.

10. Practice saying no.

> "Most modern calendars mar the sweet simplicity of our lives by reminding us that each day that passes is the anniversary of some perfectly uninteresting event."

Oscar Wilde

"Seek simplicity, and distrust it."

Alfred North Whitehead

"To be a philosopher is not merely to have subtle thoughts, not even to found a school, but so to love wisdom as to live according to its dictates, a life of simplicity, independence, magnanimity, and trust."

Walt Whitman

WALLET BIOPSY

Healthcareless

--- { **WHAT IT MEANS:**

Finding out someone's financial status and health insurance coverage before admitting them to a hospital

Unlike many medical tests, when a doctor or hospital takes a biopsy of your wallet (sometimes called a green screen), you'll want this test to be positive. Positive wallet biopsy means that a patient has the insurance or cash to cover the costs of what he needs done. Negative wallet biopsy means he doesn't. And, in America, when you've got negative wallet biopsy and you need a surgery, you might as well call a priest. The health-care industry isn't in this game for its health.

This may seem harsh, but some procedures are extremely expensive, and hospitals can't afford to do them unless they're going to get paid. A liver transplant, for example, could easily cost $400,000 for the surgery alone, and the meds run another $15,000 per year for the rest of your life. Unless you've got a positive wallet biopsy, you're not going to get a transplant. The DEATH-CARE INDUSTRY, however, will happily serve you on a budget.

✚ **FIRST COINED:** "Hospital Defends Decision Not to Treat Man with Knife in Back," Associated Press, October 1980.

WALLET SHARE

What's in Your Wallet?

--- { **WHAT IT MEANS:**

Diversifying product offerings to generate more income

At some point, trying to increase market share gets expensive. So companies go after a bigger share of your wallet. Example: Since you can only consume so many Cokes a day, a soft-drink company will try to increase its share of your wallet by selling you peanuts or chips produced by another division of its company.

Like wallet share, which is an accepted term in the marketing industry, belly share seeks to talk about the same issue—but for the food industry. However, they're still talking about wallet share, and not bragging about how much of your tummy is because of their products . . . at least, not in the marketing collateral.

➕ **FIRST COINED**: William Jackson, "These Collectors Get a Charge out of Old Credit Cards," *Business First-Columbus,* March 1990.

WAL-MARTIAN

The Invasion Is Nearly Complete

People who live more than thirty minutes from a Wal-Mart are becoming fewer every day. Oh Wal-Mart, where low price is king. In terms of sales, only Exxon-Mobil outsells this mega-corporation, which tells you a couple of key things about America. We like gas and cheap stuff. And lots of it.

Wal-World

Wal-Mart is currently the world's largest retailer as well as the world's second-largest corporation. Founded by Sam Walton in 1962 and incorporated in 1969, Wal-Mart first listed on the New York Stock Exchange in 1972. It is the largest private employer in the United States and Mexico.

Wal-Mart is also the largest grocery retailer in the America, with approximately 20 percent of the retail grocery business, and it's the largest toy seller, with an estimated 45 percent of the retail toy business, surpassing Toys "R" Us in the late 1990s.

Wal-Haters

Wal-Mart has been the target of a lot of criticism from just about everyone for its policies and business practices, including community groups, women's rights groups, grassroots organizations, labor unions, religious organizations, and environmental groups. Specific concerns include the corporation's outsourcing, how it treats employees and suppliers, wages, its hostility toward unions, insurance benefits, sexism, child labor, environmental practices, its use of public subsidies, the economic impact of stores on the communities—just about everything, really.

For many people I know, Wal-Mart and Wal-Martians have serious negative connotations. Not for me. Wal-Mart almost single-handedly has brought hyper-consumerism to Middle America. (Sure, China helped a little.) And that's probably a good thing. Without Wal-Mart, there would be even less to do outside Manhattan.

✚ **FIRST COINED:** John Lichfield, "Perot Fly in Clinton's Ointment," *The Independent,* October 1992.

WARM-CHAIR ATTRITION

Another Smoke Break?

People with warm-chair attrition have mentally, but not physically, quit their jobs. When unemployment rates rise, warm-chair attrition rises with it because employees have made a mental decision to leave, though they need the paycheck.

{ **WHAT IT MEANS:**

A productivity loss in the workplace due to employees who dislike their jobs and are waiting for the right time to quit

Several surveys indicate that 30 to 40 percent of employees are already focused on their next job rather than the one they currently have. This means that they are spending a lot of their time at work looking for their next job rather than doing what they're being paid for.

When unemployment rates rise, warm-chair attrition also rises because employees want to leave but there aren't enough opportunities out there. During these times, some employers tend to treat their employees with less care. In doing so, they're encouraging warm-chair attrition. This condition is often much more expensive than if workers leave physically, but hopefully while they're still sitting in their chairs, they'll do a little bit.

YOU MIGHT HAVE WARM-CHAIR ATTRITION IF YOU . . .

- Apply for jobs at work.
- Spend extra time in the bathroom doing nothing.
- Check your personal e-mail every five minutes.
- Pray for jury duty.
- Smoke three packs a day—and then you get home.

WEB 2.0

Internet Upgrade

In *Web 2.0,* new technologies are used to create Web sites that look

--{ **WHAT IT MEANS:**
A second phase in the evolution of the World Wide Web

and feel like desktop programs, and collaboration and communication between users is highly encouraged.

The term *Web 2.0* is everywhere these days. Though the term is pervasive, its meaning is hard to pin down. Businesses across industries and sectors use the term to describe whatever little improvements they are making to the Internet.

The *2.0* part of the name alludes to the version numbers that typically designate software upgrades, so the phrase *Web 2.0* hints at an improved form of the Web. Some suggest that technologies such as blogs, wikis, podcasts, and many others suggest a significant change in how people use the Internet.

Tim O'Reilly of O'Reilly Media, who has been cited as coining the phrase, explains *Web 2.0* with a handy little comparison in his "What Is Web 2.0?"

Old-Style Web	Web 2.0
DoubleClick	Google
AdSense Ofoto	Flickr
Akamai	BitTorrent
mp3.com	Napster
Britannica Online	Wikipedia
Personal Web sites	Blogs
E-vite	Upcoming.org and EVDB
Domain-name speculation	Search engine optimization
Page views	Cost per click
Screen scraping	Web services
Publishing	Participation
Content management systems	Wikis
Directories (taxonomy)	Tagging ("folksonomy")
Stickiness	Syndication

And if all this doesn't help you, maybe the devil can. The Devil's Dictionary 2.0 (*www.opendevil.org*) definition of Web 2.0 is:

The name given to the social and technical sophistication and maturity that mark the—Oh, screw it. Money! Money money money! Money! The money's back! Ha ha! Money!

Maybe the devil has it right this time. There's probably a lot of money to be made in this Web 2.0 thing, whatever it is. And, if you didn't blow your wad on the Web 1.0 fallout, maybe this time will be different. Or maybe we've all forgotten, and history will repeat itself yet again.

➕ **FIRST COINED**: "Top Internet Industry Leaders Assemble at Web 2.0 Conference to Drive Innovation in the Internet Economy," *Business Wire,* May 2004.

WELCHISM

Lean and Mean Management Machine

⌐--{ **WHAT IT MEANS:**

A business management fad based on the writings of Chairman Jack (former GE exec Jack Welch)

Jack Welch was chairman and CEO of GE between 1981 and 2001. During his tenure, GE increased its market capitalization by over $400 billion. He remains a highly regarded figure in business circles due to his innovative management strategies and leadership style.

Throughout the 1980s, Welch worked to make GE a more competitive company. He tried to get rid of inefficiency by cutting inventories and dismantling the giant GE bureaucracy.

Welch believed that a company should be either the leader or the runner-up in an industry or get out of it. His strategy was later adopted by other CEOs across the business world. See FAD SURFING.

GREAT WELCHISMS
- "An overburdened, overstretched executive is the best executive because he or she doesn't have the time to meddle, to deal in trivia, to bother people."
- "I was afraid of the Internet . . . because I couldn't type."

W

- "If GE's strategy of investment in China is wrong, it represents a loss of a billion dollars, perhaps a couple of billion dollars. If it is right, it is the future of this company for the next century."
- "Giving people self-confidence is by far the most important thing that I can do. Because then they will act."
- "The Internet is the Viagra of big business."

WHISPER CIRCUIT

This Is Gonna Be Big!

WHAT IT MEANS:
A forum in which people exchange rumors, gossip, and innuendo

In the financial world, the whisper circuit is about the size of Jupiter. Financial message boards are a notorious whisper circuit, and blogs are another. If you run with a finance crowd (whether savvy or inept), people all think they know something that will put them ahead of the curve.

Next time you hear someone say a stock is "about to make a big move," be sure to ask, "Up or down, stupid?"

TYPICAL RUMORS ON THE WHISPER CIRCUIT

- "They're about to file a lawsuit against the CEO."
- "Britney Spears is the new spokeswoman."
- "Recent studies suggest that everyone who has ever used the product has dropped dead."
- "Google's got its eye on them."
- "Warren Buffett says they're a buy."

Some famous people, having had to deal with one form of whisper circuit or another, have made very astute comments about it.

"It isn't what they say about you, it's what they whisper."

Errol Flynn

"People should be more concerned with the whispering of their conscience than the whispers of others."

Gregory Bergman

"I wasn't kissing her, I was whispering in her mouth."

Chico Marx

⊕ **FIRST COINED:** "The Ear," *Washington Post,* October 1981.

WORK RAGE

Rage Against the Machine

In America, school and office shootings are becoming somewhat of a tradition, like Thanksgiving

WHAT IT MEANS:
Anger expressed in the workplace by an employee who has been mistreated or fired

or March Madness. From Columbine to the Xerox killings in Hawaii to Virginia Tech, large-scale massacres are occurring at an alarming rate.

What can be done about this epidemic? In the office, employers fire people on Friday, hoping that fired employees will consider their weekend plans before reacting violently. But while this may temporarily quell their rage, it won't stop them from coming back on Monday and gunning their ex-coworkers down in cold blood.

As a real solution to this problem, some call for more gun control. Some call for stricter anti-bullying rules in the office and the classroom, and some call for the sensationalist news networks to stop exacerbating the problem by turning these murderers into celebrities. Still others claim that it's a cultural problem and that there's not much we can do.

W

However, there is something that *you* can do to protect yourself at work. If a coworker is acting a little nutty, make sure to tell your boss and then take a few DUVET DAYS to lay low.

IS YOUR COWORKER ABOUT TO SNAP?

- He spends his lunch break reading *Guns, Bullets, and Explosives.*
- She can be described as "quiet, polite, and shy."
- He hasn't been laid since college. He graduated in 1993.
- When you click on her MySpace page, one of Adolf Hitler's speeches starts to play.
- He recently converted to Wahhabism.
- Her screen name on Yahoo is officekiller666.
- His favorite song is "Helter Skelter."
- She has a *Cooking for Cannibals* book on her desk.
- He always wears surgical gloves, a hockey mask, and a long, flowing black coat.
- She comes in early, leaves late, and never has a problem with anyone.

➕ **FIRST COINED:** Ian Burrell and Adrian Levy, "Office Workers Turn Violent in 'Suit Wars'," *Sunday Times,* November 1995.

XEROX SUBSIDY

Office Supplies

Your office is filled with things you could use around the house. Because of this, your home is full

> { **WHAT IT MEANS:**
> Using your company's printer or copy machine for personal use

of things you've borrowed (the taken-without-asking-and-will-never-give-back type of borrowing). But one thing that's difficult to borrow is the copy machine. And while you're not sure it would look good in your anteroom, if you could get away with taking it, you would. Who wouldn't?

At ten cents or so a page—not to mention having to hang out under the fluorescent lights with all those college students, homeless, and facsimile specialists—the local copy shop is not where you want to spend your spare time.

Since It's Not Bolted Down . . .

Plus, even if you have your own copy machine or printer, why waste your own ink and paper? Your boss will never know the difference. Okay, not all of us are OFFICE CREEPERS, but most of us take a little here and there. According to one study by Lawyers.com, some 58 percent of workers lift supplies. Of those, 77 percent stole pens, 44 percent stole sticky notes, 40 percent took paper clips, and 2 percent admitted to stealing decorations and furniture. What's more, 0.05 percent stole their boss's spouse and 0.01 percent stole their boss's car. (The last two numbers are purely my own speculation.)

YETTIE

A Different Kind of Abomination

{ WHAT IT MEANS:

A young, entrepreneurial technocrat

Not to be confused with the yeti, a mythical apelike animal said to inhabit the Himalayas. These creatures have probably never been to Nepal, Bhutan, or Tibet (though they may have gone to a Free Tibet gathering). No, the yettie is something else entirely—though you may wish that these nerds were a figment of people's imagination too.

There are still a lot of yetties around, but if you remember the late 1990s, it seemed like every kid with a PC was rich and nerdy. In 2000, a book was written on the yettie, entitled *A Field Guide to the Yettie: America's Young, Entrepreneurial Technocrats.* It became all but obsolete when, just a few short months later, order was restored to the universe and the dot-com bubble burst. Now, most yetties are, once again, playing video games and working at fast-food restaurants. There they should remain.

YOTTABYTE

Size Is Relative

A yottabyte is about 2 million gigabytes. That's 10,000 times bigger than your average hard drive today. Not too long ago, a gigabyte

WHAT IT MEANS:

A number that equals 2 to the power of 80—a million trillion megabytes (roughly 1,208,925, 819,614,629,174,706,176)

was huge. Before that, megabytes and kilobytes reigned, and now they all seem like kid sizes. Terabytes are probably not too far away from our home computers, and in no time, we'll download gigabytes of files in minutes. With a yottabyte, the Super Big Gulp of the data world, you could hold the entire contents of the Library of Congress, YouTube, and Capital Records—and don't forget Vivid Video. What an organizational nightmare.

Need for Speed

To handle this much data, computers and Internet connections will need to improve just as dramatically. As it stands now, it would take over a trillion years to download a yottabyte. Too long for anything I've recently seen on the Net. And, if computers become that fast and that smart, will they turn evil? Do we have a *Terminator* or *Matrix*-style future ahead of us?

Unit	Power of 2	Actual Bytes
Kilo	10	1,024
Mega	20	1,048,576
Giga	30	1,073,741,824
Tera	40	1,099,511,627,776
Peta	50	1,125,899,906,842,624
Exa	60	1,152,921,504,606,846,976
Zetta	70	1,180,591,620,717,411,303,424
Yotta	80	1,208,925,819,614,629,174,706,176

ZEN MAIL

Finding Zen Online

Ever get annoyed when someone sends you an e-mail that says nothing? Don't. Take this opportunity to seek enlightenment, grasshopper.

WHAT IT MEANS:
Net jargon for an e-mail message without text or attachments

What Would Buddha Do?

Of the fifty or so e-mails I get every day, they break down something like this:

Spam: 72%
Personal: 8%
Business: 19%
Zen: 1%

In this world of information overload, do what Buddha would when you get the chance. Spend a minute staring at that blank e-mail, meditate, take a sip of coffee and get back to work. This especially applies to writers, who must learn to find peace and inspiration in blank screens.

BUDDHA QUOTES TO PONDER OVER YOUR NEXT ZEN MAIL:

- "Believe nothing, no matter where you read it, or who said it, no matter if I have said it, unless it agrees with your own reason and your own common sense."
- "A dog is not considered a good dog because he is a good barker. A man is not considered a good man because he is a good talker."
- "Ennui has made more gamblers than avarice, more drunkards than thirst, and perhaps as many suicides as despair."
- "He who loves fifty people has fifty woes; he who loves no one has no woes."
- "There are only two mistakes one can make along the road to truth; not going all the way, and not starting."

ZERO DRAG

WHAT IT MEANS:
An employee with few personal responsibilities who can work long hours, travel frequently, or be called in on little notice

Life's a Drag

Sure your boss, like mine, says the job is nine to five and a little extra when needed, but what that bloodsucker really wants is for you to spend every waking moment of your life working and thinking about work. To that tick, a spouse is a drag; kids are a drag; even your cat is a drag. These things take away from your focus on work and slow you down.

Nothing makes a boss happier than when she sees the resume of a young, smart, experienced, low-drag applicant. Make sure to let her believe that even if it's not the case. If she dumps you after the fact, at least you can collect unemployment insurance. Or if you're lucky, a nice discrimination lawsuit could let you start your own business.

IS YOUR LIFE A DRAG?

- For each thirty minutes of commute time, add a point.
- If you're married, add a point.
- For each girl/boyfriend you have within 100 miles of your job, add a point.
- For each girl/boy friend you have outside 100 miles of your job, add a half point.
- For each child you have who lives with you, add a point.
- For each pet you have that weighs over one pound, add a point.
- For each club, association, or support group you frequent, add one point.

My score is 1. Low drag. My boss still hates me. *C'est la vie.*

✚ **FIRST COINED:** Po Bronson, "Instant Company," *New York Times,* July 1999.

ZEROTASKING

Absolute Zero

A funny word that takes its form from *multitasking, zerotasking* is

{ WHAT IT MEANS:

To do nothing or to have nothing to do at work

the kind of thing you do at work when you are ridiculously tired, insanely hung over, or tremendously irritated at your boss.

Other words for this common phenomenon in the workplace include *daydreaming, procrastinating,* or sometimes even PRO-CRASTURBATION. Zerotasking is probably more common than most employers would like to admit.

The Zen of Zero
There is a Zen-like quality to zerotasking. It's meditative, and it's peaceful . . . until you get fired. Unlike MULTISLACKING, zero-tasking doesn't involve even the pretense of being productive.

Some say a little zerotasking may actually be beneficial to both employees as well as employers. Joyce Brothers, one of America's leading family psychologists and advice columnists, says, "No matter how much pressure you feel at work, if you could find ways to relax for at least five minutes every hour, you'd be more productive."

Too bad the boss won't go for that.

➕ **FIRST COINED:** This word was first printed in the caption of a *New Yorker* cartoon, which pictured a very relaxed man plopped in a comfortable chair.

ZIP CODE MARKETING

{ **WHAT IT MEANS:**
A marketing campaign aimed at a specific zip code

Everyone's into Zip
Ever wonder why the salesperson at Radio Shack asks you, "What's your zip code?" He's not necessarily coming on to you, nor is he a stalker. But Radio Shack's corporate marketing team is. Well, kinda. The information they gather is used to determine areas with desired demographic or economic attributes. For example: an area populated by affluent, well-educated families.

Smells Like Profits and Bacon

Let's say we're selling bacon-scented candles, and our marketing research has determined that people between the ages of thirty-five and fifty go crazy for them. But our bacon-scented candles are premium, so our team knows that people whose household income is in the top 10 percent are our customers. With zip-code data, we see where these people congregate, and we sell our candles there. This improves our sales per store, per employee, and per square foot—pushing up our revenue, while keeping our expenses down. If the zip-code data is comprehensive enough, we could keep our bacon-scented candles out of areas where people just won't buy them, despite how good they smell. Places like:

1. Tel Aviv
2. Queens
3. South Florida
4. Spain before the Inquisition
5. Hollywood

➕ **FIRST COINED**: Mike Drexler, "How Newspapers Can Survive Mid-Life Crisis," *Marketing & Media Decisions,* February 1983.

ZOMBIE

The Living Dead

WHAT IT MEANS:
A bankrupt company that operates in the face of a pending merger or closure

In fiction, a zombie is a walking, brain-sucking corpse of a recently deceased person whose body has become reanimated. In finance, it's a company ready to be gobbled up by another one or be buried alive. The employees of the zombie company aren't infected. They don't dress in rags, have missing limbs, or walk with arms stretched out. They are, however, updating their resumes and shopping for a new suit to interview in.

SIGNS THAT YOU MIGHT HAVE A ZOMBIE IN YOUR PORTFOLIO:

- Expenditures are huge; revenues are tiny.
- Staff turnover is high and increasing rapidly.
- There's a serious lack of demand for the product or service.
- Liabilities tremendously outweigh assets.
- Financial statements don't accurately reflect the cash position.
- Credit rating is dropping quickly.
- Financing becomes nearly impossible.

Sell or Hold? Well . . .

Of course, there are examples of companies bouncing back from dire situations. And, if the market has already priced this in, there may be no reason to sell. If, for example, you've already lost 75 percent of your investment, you have to ask yourself whether or not you can stand losing more. A buyout or revitalization could add value to your investment, eliminating some or all of your losses, but that may not happen. So I suggest you do what I do to make all of life's toughest, most important decisions: Flip a coin.

Appendix

Major Sources

About.com
Answers.com
Buzzwhack.com
Dangerouslogic.com
The Devil's Dictionary 2.0
Investopedia.com
Neologisms.us
Putlearningfirst.com
Wikipedia.org
Wordspy.com
Zoom.co.uk